Peter Hollins is a bestselling author, human psychology researcher, and a dedicated student of the human condition. He possesses a BS in psychology and has worked with dozens of people from all walks of life.

He enjoys hiking with his family, drinking craft beers and attempting to paint. He is based in Seattle, Washington.

THE BRAIN MECHANIC

Think Smarter, Not Harder

PETER HOLLINS

RUPA

Published by
Rupa Publications India Pvt. Ltd 2024
7/16, Ansari Road, Daryaganj
New Delhi 110002

Sales Centres:
Bengaluru Chennai
Hyderabad Jaipur Kathmandu
Kolkata Mumbai Prayagraj

The views and opinions expressed in this book are the author's own and the facts are as reported by him which have been verified to the extent possible, and the publishers are not in any way liable for the same.

P-ISBN: 978-93-5520-941-2
E-ISBN: 978-93-5702-404-4

First impression 2024

10 9 8 7 6 5 4 3 2 1

The moral right of the author has been asserted.

Printed in India

CONTENTS

1

NEUROFITNESS

When you break your leg, you go to the doctor. When you experience depression, you go to the psychiatrist or psychologist (maybe). And when you're having an existential crisis, you might even consult a spiritual teacher or life coach. Though we like to divide ourselves up into "body, mind, and spirit," the truth is that human beings are complex *wholes*, and "mental health" is not different from "physical health" or even "spiritual health." It's all just health in the end.

It's obvious when you think about it: There is no mind without a brain, and your brain is as much a physical part of you as your legs or spleen or immune system. It doesn't matter how high-minded your ideals, how strong your will, how lofty your dreams—if your physical being is compromised, then you can never reach your highest cognitive or intellectual potential. Although it might seem counterintuitive, one of the best ways to boost not just mental health but your brain's ability to do what it does best (think!) is to take care of your *entire organism*—and that includes your physical body. Take care of your physical fitness, and your brain inevitably benefits, and vice versa—build a strong, healthy brain, and it will in turn help you maintain your physical health.

This might seem an obvious point to some, but for others, we're dedicated to all systems working hard, pushing the boundaries, and burning the midnight oil. This simply won't work because we're not steel and oil machines that can be pushed in that manner. In this chapter, we'll talk about just how to prepare the body so that the mind can follow. The way we can increase our neurofitness actually has little to do with activities involving the brain; rather, it's about actions that will benefit the brain as a side effect. You will notice this theme throughout the book as well.

It's a point that bears repeating: As we understand our physiology and neurology better and better, it becomes clear that the brain adapts up or down to our daily tasks and lifestyle (and not to supposed brain training programs that purport to increase your intelligence).

So how can we make sure it is adapting in a way we want?

Get Moving and Sweating

Physical fitness can often be defined by how active you are, or how much exercise you engage in. And to be honest, that's not a bad metric to use. The vast majority of us could stand to exercise a little more than we currently are, even beyond the purposes of this book to boost our brain functioning.

Of course, it's been shown that exercise assists with general cognitive functioning, including memory. But sometimes when we talk about the benefits of exercise, it becomes difficult to separate what helps the brain versus what supports a healthy lifestyle in general. These elements are too intertwined to bother separating, but for instance, the body reacts to exercise by improving insulin response, reducing inflammation, boosting flexibility, increasing bone density, and becoming more resistant to injury or illness. Additionally, exercise makes you happier through the release of endorphins, it increases your self-esteem and confidence, and it even reduces the symptoms of stress and anxiety.

But you probably knew those benefits already. When you exercise, what exactly happens in the brain?

One notable study was conducted at Radboud University in the Netherlands. Male and female subjects took a memory test, and then one-third of them exercised immediately after the test, one-third exercised four hours after the test, and the remaining third did not exercise after the test. The subjects were collected two days later to repeat the same memory test, and the group who exercised four hours after the initial test performed the best without fail. It appeared that exercise was effective in helping the brain stabilize and store the memory.

This study seems fairly conclusive in itself, but it's just part of a larger body of literature that shows surprising effects that transfer from below the neck to above it, so to speak. In another study done at the University of British Columbia, researchers found that aerobic exercise, the kind that gets your heart and your sweat glands pumping, also appears to boost the size of the hippocampus. Of course, this is the brain area involved in memory and learning.

In another study, researchers concluded that even among people who did not meet the activity guidelines, each hour of light-intensity physical activity and achieving 7,500 steps or more daily was associated with higher total brain volume. This was equivalent to approximately 1.4 to 2.2 years less brain aging—or fighting the natural rate of brain mass attrition due to aging. It's pretty important to note that resistance training, such as weightlifting or balance training, did not have the same result. You need to get your sweat on and raise your heart rate to achieve these benefits.

Most studies on exercise and memory tend to focus on elderly populations and how to prevent cognitive decline. In the end, we discover that the brain is very much "use it or lose it." In a 2019 study, 454 older adults underwent yearly physical exams and cognitive tests for twenty years and agreed to donate their brains for research when they died. The participants were given accelerometers, which tracked their movement and physical activity around the clock.

Those who moved more scored better on the memory and thinking tests, and every increase in physical activity by one standard deviation was associated with a thirty-one percent lower risk of dementia, the researchers reported. The association between physical activity and cognitive function remained consistent even after the authors accounted for the participants' brain pathology and whether they had dementia, according to the study.

Even though elderly populations will greatly benefit from staving off cognitive decline, there are marked effects for everyone else below the age of sixty, and in fact, as young as twenty years old. These new studies come from Yaakov Stern and his colleagues at Columbia University, and they found exercise increased executive functions, which are generally thinking skills that we use in our everyday lives, including our ability to regulate our behavior, pay attention, organize, plan, and achieve goals. Stern also found exercise caused physical changes in the thickness of certain areas of the brain, similar to prior findings involving the hippocampus.

The participants were then randomized to undertake either a six-month aerobic exercise training program, or a six-month control program of stretching and core-strengthening exercises. Participants were all tested for cognitive parameters, including executive function, processing speed, language, attention, and episodic memory, before the exercise programs were initiated, and then at twelve and twenty-four weeks. They also underwent MRI brain scans to identify any changes in brain structure.

By the end of the six-month intervention, individuals who did aerobic exercise increased their executive function test scores by 0.5 points, which was statistically significant when compared with the 0.25-point improvement shown by the stretching and toning group. At forty years of age, the improvement in thinking skills was 0.28 standard deviation units higher among those who did aerobic exercise, compared with those who did stretching and toning. At age sixty, the difference was 0.596 standard deviation units higher, the researchers reported.

The researchers stated, "Since a difference of 0.5 standard deviations is equivalent to twenty years of age-related difference in performance on these tests, the people who exercised were testing as if they were about ten years younger at age forty and about twenty years younger at age sixty."

Interestingly, brain imaging at the start of the study and at week twenty-four suggested that aerobic exercise training was also associated with structural changes in particular regions of the brain: increased cortical thickness in the left caudal middle frontal area.

The message is clear and resounding and really summed up in the title of this section: get sweating, get out of breath, and raise your heart rate to a point where you need to rest afterward. Both directly and indirectly, you're doing your brain good.

And we haven't even mentioned BDNF yet. Exercise is instrumental in the production of a brain protein called FNDC5, which eventually releases brain-derived neurotrophic factor (BDNF). BDNF has been shown to aid general brain functioning and memory processing by preserving existing brain cells, promoting the growth of new brain cells, and encouraging overall brain growth. Human brains tend to shrink when we grow older, but exercise, which creates BDNF, can literally increase the size of your brain.

The presence of BDNF is especially supportive of long-term memory. Most BDNF activity occurs in the brain areas most correlated with high-level cognition, learning, and recall—the hippocampus, cortex, and basal forebrain. BDNF can also help proper sleep regulation and (though this is not a promise) can curb excessive appetite, which could lead to marginal weight loss. Conversely, the *lack* of BDNF can cause depression, and people suffering from Parkinson's disease tend to have low levels of the protein.

Researcher Joyce Gomes-Osman reviewed studies that associated exercise with different brain functions. Her goal was to find what "doses" of exercise were most effective for certain types of cognitive function. While Gomes-Osman stressed that there wasn't a "magic number" that will unfailingly promote greater brain function, she did determine that elderly people who managed one hour of exercise three days per week showed the greatest improvement in brain functioning and speed.

At this point, you probably don't need any more convincing as to the virtues of exercise for your brain, but let's leave with just one final vital piece of information. Your brain has the highest oxygen requirement of any organ in your body, up to twenty percent of your entire body's usage. When you improve your cardiovascular system through exercise and ensure that blood is pumping more efficiently through your arteries, you will have greater access to oxygen. It's the same with water—the brain is, on average, composed of seventy percent water, and exercise typically makes you more aware of hydration. Feed your hungry brain by making sure its supply systems are optimized.

There is one small caveat that comes with an issue few of us will ever encounter: *too much* exercise. As you'll read later when we discuss stress, when exercise becomes so excessive and strenuous that it begins to create an anxious mental state, whether from burnout or discomfort, then your neurofitness goes straight down the toilet. Likewise, overtraining can weaken the immune system and create harmful inflammation that may completely wipe out any potential exercise benefits.

However, overall, the maxim of *healthy body, healthy mind* holds true.

Bend and Stretch (Your Brain)

We've talked about how the body directly affects the mind, but what about training the two systems in a synergistic manner? One increasingly popular method that might have sprung to mind is yoga, which has ancient roots as a complete system of development and maintenance of body, mind, and spirit all at once. I promise this discussion isn't going to verge into "woo-woo" territory, but rather will look at the simple scientific evidence.

By now, yoga has been extensively studied for decades for its effect on mood, well-being, and overall physical health. But more recently, researchers are discovering noteworthy cognitive benefits to getting out the yoga mat and limbering up for some downward-facing dog. Yoga postures, breathing techniques, and the cultivated focus on mindful presence in each moment can have subtle but profound effects on the way your brain works. They can also strengthen the body-mind connection and promote a deeper sense of self-awareness and self-regulation.

Whether it's just a weekly class or a more dedicated long-term practice, yoga helps your brain health in several different ways. When researchers look at those practitioners who have consistently done yoga over a long period, they discover that their brains are noticeably different from those who have never practiced. In fact, one of the chief findings is that yoga may protect our brains against the effects of aging.

Sara Lazar and her team found in 2005 that meditation actually reduced the occurrence of *cortical thinning*, which is closely related to degenerative illness and aging, such as

Alzheimer's and Parkinson's disease. The prefrontal cortex is associated with complex decision-making, executive functioning, impulse control, and emotional regulation. People with more gray matter in this region of the brain make fewer mistakes in experimental cognitive tests. If yoga practitioners have thicker prefrontal cortices, it stands to reason that all that extra gray matter protects them from neurological decline in later years, giving them greater cognitive control and mastery than those who never do yoga.

Does this mean that these yogis are literally smarter than those who don't practice yoga? That would be going too far, but based on Lazar's work, we can say that practitioners may be sharper at senior ages.

Similar research by Chantal Villemure and colleagues in 2015 tried to see whether the same was true of those practicing yoga long-term (that means forty-five minutes three or four times a week over at least three years) and found that yoga did in fact seem to protect the brain against age-related degeneration and brain disease. Those who did yoga had more gray matter overall, including larger prefrontal cortices and limbic systems—those regions involved in emotion, memory, and stress regulation.

Several other studies corroborate these findings, and in particular it would seem frequent yoga protects the hippocampus from aging. Since the hippocampus is also the region of the brain responsible for how we manage stress and process our world emotionally, making sure it's healthy means we boost our overall mood and ward off mental illness and perhaps even memory problems. In fact, those with major depression or mental disorders like PTSD often show shrinking of the hippocampus. What better proof that mental health is really not so different from physical health?

In general, scientists now understand that stress can reduce hippocampal (and overall brain) volume, but also that a person with a smaller hippocampus is more prone to developing certain mental disorders. So how do we know which caused which? The relationship between the size of these various parts of the brain and your mental state is likely complex, but one thing is clear: When you take care of your brain health, you reap cognitive, emotional, and intellectual rewards while fending off the onset of age-related degenerative diseases like Alzheimer's. This is turn can feed back into physical health, with physiological and behavioral changes mutually reinforcing one another.

Granted, many of these studies are ongoing and their results should be interpreted with a grain of salt. Small sample sizes and cross-sectional designs means it's a little harder to tell if yoga alone is indeed the cause of the findings—it may be true that those who naturally have more gray matter find themselves doing more yoga, for whatever reason. There may also be a third variable, like socio-economic status or education, that affects both the likelihood of doing yoga and having greater cortical volume.

Further, there's the question of what aspect of yoga actually benefits our wayward brains and causes relaxation; is it the physical act alone with the increased blood flow, BDNF, and rise in endorphins after the fact, or is it rather the mental space and clarity that one practices while engaging in such a peaceful activity? Later in this book, we'll explore some interesting evidence for the value of stretching, since it enhances endorphin production and protects the brain—whether you're doing a professional downward-facing dog asana or not! Regardless, few would argue that taking the time to breathe, center yourself, and stretch a few times a week could fail to have benefits, especially when practiced over years. For some people, yoga is primarily a spiritual or even social discipline, and it's *this* that ultimately provides the benefits.

However, as we ponder the specific causes for these improvements, do we really need to get caught up in the "why" when we have a very clear "how"? This type of analysis might cause too much paralysis, when sometimes we can just start *doing* rather than *contemplating*. It turns out that this action-based mindset is key to achieving the entirety of the life you want, not just an improved and optimized brain.

What remains to be seen in future research is whether the promising effects described here can be repeated on wider scales, or indeed if those with reduced hippocampal volume or gray matter can actually reverse their condition by doing yoga. If so, it may be more common in the future to find age-related therapies leaning heavily toward yoga and meditation instead of chronic medication. In the meantime, though, there is nothing to be lost by introducing a little yoga into your own routine.

Ask any devoted yogi, and they may wax lyrical about the benefits—even beyond those that could be measured quantitatively by brain studies. Proponents will describe the sense of calm and present-mindedness that comes with regular practice. It's a form of self-care, a way to quiet a busy mind, and a wonderful method for nurturing that mind-body connection and developing body awareness. Yoga is like moving meditation for some.

Yoga is great for stress reduction and maintaining flexibility. But over and above all this, it simply *feels* good. In this chaotic and overstimulated world, many people find enormous benefit to simply drawing in fresh breath, stilling the mind, and getting into their bodies. This is something we will certainly revisit when we talk about mindfulness and meditation as a supplement to our daily routines.

It could be this ability to reconnect with the body that's key. We all live in a hyper-cerebral world, surrounded by noisy distractions and abstract concepts, symbols, and language, and most likely we work in occupations that center on monotonous mental and intellectual labor. We spend days sitting or driving, browsing online, watching TV—in effect living in the world as though we were merely giant brains propped up by the life support systems we call our bodies. We may live this way for decades, only engaging with our bodies or emotions when they fail to behave as we think they should, or if we fall ill.

But a more holistic perspective reminds us that we *are* our bodies. Nothing can convince you more of the primacy of your physical being than falling seriously ill. In that situation, it doesn't matter how much personal development you've indulged in, or how dazzling your career is. We live in a world dominated by the brain. But, paradoxically, it's in cutting our cognitive selves off from our bodies that we actually undermine our ability to think well, make decisions, solve problems, or really create.

Express Yourself Physically

We know that any activity producing a modicum of sweat is going to have surprising neurological benefits. But another beneficial, perhaps neglected, practice is *dancing*. Dancing is exercise, but it is not goal directed, not arbitrary and abstract in the way that a bicep curl or a ten-second sprint is. Dancing can be lyrical, expressive, joyful, sociable, exhilarating—it's the ability to move the body poetically and to gain pleasure from the sheer privilege of being alive and able to move and breathe.

Dancing is a hobby, a passion, and an art, but it can be so much more than that. Rhythmically moving the body to sounds and responding dynamically to music is not just fun, it is extremely good for your health, too. When you dance, you're engaging in cardiovascular exercise, you're breathing deeply, and maybe you're even breaking a sweat. We know this second part is always beneficial to our mental and cognitive health, but the part about expression and creativity cannot be understated. Engaging in artistic activity lifts you emotionally.

In fact, dance is increasingly employed as a therapy for alleviating the symptoms of depression, anxiety, and other mental illnesses. Dancing is the whole package—when you move this way, you're engaging your emotional, physical, and mental self. Your body moves and your heart beats. You smile and feel great, uplifted by the beat and enjoying your partner dancing with you, if you have one.

If you're taking a dance class, maybe you have to focus on dance moves and pay close attention to coordinate your motor functions properly so you can execute complex movements right on time with the music. And, if you're a real dance enthusiast, you may even experience an ecstatic moment of selflessness, of total flow and absorption in the moment, more closely resembling prayer or deep meditation than a boring old treadmill workout.

In dance/movement therapy (DMT), the physical movement of the body is understood as a language in its own right, able to communicate and express our experience just as well as words. Dance is a way to remind ourselves that we all possess this vocabulary. The interesting thing is that when we reconnect with our physical selves this way and "change channels," our cognitive functioning only benefits. Stress levels are reduced, endorphins are released, and we reap the emotional, social, and even spiritual benefits of having explored our full range of human expression. Along with this come feelings of freedom, liberation, confidence, and self-assuredness.

Multiple studies have shown that dance can improve memory and general cognitive function, specifically boosting spatial and working memory. Verghese and his colleagues at Albert Einstein College of Medicine even found a seventy-six percent drop in risk of dementia onset when their participants danced regularly. Other studies show that dancing can also reduce the symptoms of depression. We already know that maintaining physical activity as we age is vital for keeping motor and mental skills intact, but a more holistic practice like dancing can also boost mood, perceptual abilities, memory, and other cognitive skills. On top of all that, it can be a deeply rewarding artistic or social practice.

It might seem like a tall order, but dancing does all of this by stimulating nerve growth factors in the brain (BDNF, as we have covered). These factors are responsible for the health of sensory neurons. Essentially, dancing enhances the connections between the cerebral hemispheres—the left and right parts of the brain—and thus boosts neuroplasticity, which in turn bolsters the ability to make new neural connections. Naturally, this is great news for anyone trying to enhance their ability to change and adapt their brains—i.e., learning new things!

Though dance is now being used to treat degenerative neurological conditions like stroke and cerebral palsy, you can reap the benefits too. Don't worry if you're uncoordinated or feel like you're not "good" at dancing. All that's required is that you *move* (it won't hurt to try to enjoy yourself, either) in a way that satisfies you emotionally—that makes you feel free-spirited and uninhibited.

If you're studying for an exam, you may get more benefit from taking a dance break than trying to cram an extra twenty minutes in. In this way, you are activating different parts of your brain, increasing blood flow to your brain, creating a vivid memory, and simply waking up.

If you're shy, put on some loud music when you're home alone, draw the curtains, and let go in complete darkness. You could actively imagine your brain making all its wonderful connections between the music, your breathing, your heart rate, and the movement of your muscles. Make it a "moving meditation," or simply kick back and do whatever you want, so long as it makes you feel good. You may find yourself energized both physically and psychologically by the time you sit back down to study again.

A long-term dance practice may be as beneficial as yoga. Join a dance group you like the look of—why not try a class in ballet, tap, salsa, ballroom, hip hop, or something completely different, like Tahitian hula. If choreography is not your idea of fun, try freeform dance classes that encourage expression and spontaneous movement, like Biodanza.

This is movement that's less about choreography and more about lived, real physical expression in the moment. You forget about the office, about your worries, about everything, and simply sink into the music, letting your body take the lead for once. Yes, you may feel silly at first, but once you drop the self-consciousness, your brain will thank you. If that's a little too out there for you, why not just head out with some friends to a place where you can simply feel the music and get lost in a crowd? "Ecstatic dancing" may sound very serious indeed, but it's nothing more than taking a few deep breaths, feeling the music inside, and allowing your body to respond to it as it will.

Like with yoga, you may find it tempting to try to pinpoint exactly what part of the act is truly blessing your brain. Is it the artistic creativity, the sense of liberation, the physical sweat aspect, or the emotional satiation that often follows? Well, it's all of them, and they all work together. The body is the brain, and we forget this at our own peril.

If boosting your brain health is your goal, which form of physical exercise should you choose? Well, at its most basic, *any* form of movement is better than being sedentary, but beyond that, the choice is yours. If yoga feels like a boring, pressure-filled obligation that you don't really enjoy, then don't force it. Likewise, if you prefer to get your heart rate up by hiking and wouldn't be caught dead in a CrossFit gym, that's okay too!

Your body was born to move, and your brain is happiest

when your body is doing just that. Pick an activity that stimulates and challenges you but isn't too difficult that you feel demotivated or overwhelmed. Pick something that fits your lifestyle, your stage of life, your skillset, your preferences, and the needs and limits of your unique body.

Takeaways:

- Physical fitness begets neurofitness. It may be tempting to separate the two, but in truth, they are inexorably linked to your optimized thinking and functioning. We may not be able to specifically train the brain, but by training our bodies in specific ways, we can effect the changes that we want.

- The first step to physical fitness is to work up a sweat on a regular basis. Of note, this should be aerobic exercise that gets your blood pumping and your heart rate up. This also increases the blood flow to your brain, kicks off a host of metabolic and hormonal changes, and energizes you. It's been shown that aerobic exercise can increase the size of parts of our brains responsible for higher cognitive functions and memory, and can even fight cognitive decline and brain diseases. The brain is a hungry, hungry organ, so we should make sure the systems that feed it are optimized and healthy.

- Yoga and dance have also been found to be effective in increasing neurofitness. This may be surprising because they are not strictly seen as aerobic activities. Sure, dance can be as strenuous as running, but part of the benefit with these modes of exercise is the ability to express emotions in a gratifying way. This is demonstrated by the fact that these modes do a lot to battle and prevent depression and anxiety. How often are we able to truly unplug, let go, express ourselves, or reflect upon our lives? The links are not one hundred percent definitive, but the benefits have been documented time after time, so perhaps the "why" is not as important as the "how."

- Emotional wellness and calmness are a train of thought that makes one think of mindfulness and meditation, and it turns out that these methods do provide some of the same avenues to brain boosting. The restorative power of dance and yoga actually uncovers another rabbit hole we will dive into later: self-care.

2

NEUROTRANSMITTER FINE-TUNING

Understanding DOSE Chemicals

We've looked at the brain on a structural level and seen how it's part and parcel of our entire physical being. In this chapter, let's zoom in and look at the *functioning* of the brain—which is mediated and manifested by the release of certain brain chemicals called neurotransmitters. These are the brain's electrochemical messengers.

It's strange to realize that every one of your thoughts, feelings, and beliefs originates and reveals itself as a chemical in your brain. The way you communicate, solve problems, set goals, and perceive yourself comes down not just to this or that brain chemical, but also to their overall relative proportion. Most cakes contain flour, eggs, and milk, but the relative amount of each of these ingredients determines whether the cake is good or not. Similarly, all human brains contain these same neurochemicals, but their relative amounts make a big, big difference!

The acronym DOSE stands for the four most influential

brain chemicals (neurotransmitters) that impact our overall wellbeing:

- Dopamine
- Oxytocin
- Serotonin
- Endorphins

Simply put, these are the four key players in making us feel happy, and the logic goes that if we can moderate and balance their levels in our brains, we can boost our feelings of happiness.

In his *Psychology Today* article, Christopher Bergland ("The Neurochemicals of Happiness," 2019) explains that certain drugs can crudely alter our DOSE levels, but that scientific research is increasingly showing that we have more control over these chemicals than was first believed . . . and without resorting to chemical manipulation.

Let's take a closer look at each neurochemical and what its role is.

Oxytocin

This neurotransmitter is all about human connection and bonding. It's released any time we are close to others, and because it feels so good, it has encouraged our species to be pro-social and empathetic. Oxytocin has found to be high in pregnant women during and after labor (the chemical stimulates uterine contractions as well as breastfeeding) and in men and women during orgasm. Interestingly, it's low in teenagers and those living isolated lifestyles.

This "love hormone," which is released any time we bond, cuddle, or have sex, is associated with better mental health, monogamy, more satisfying relationships, and characteristics like loyalty and trustworthiness.

It's not as simple as that, though. Oxytocin is sometimes thought of as an emotional "amplifier"—while it increases sociability to those we trust, it may actually increase feelings of distrust to those not in our inner circle. And though the chemical can sharpen our social memories, a 2010 PNAS study found that it just as readily strengthened negative social memories as pleasant ones (Bartz et al., *Effects of Oxytocin on Recollections of Maternal Care*).

In this experiment, men were given oxytocin, then asked to write about their mothers. Those with positive memories wrote positively, but those with dysfunctional ones only described more vividly that dysfunction.

Clearly, it's not a question of whether a neurotransmitter is good or bad, healthy or unhealthy. Rather it's about finding an *optimal* level of oxytocin.

You'll know your levels are too low if you struggle to feel affection for others, lack empathy, or don't enjoy social interactions and communication with others. Low oxytocin can also result in a kind of mechanical, loveless sex life or the inability to orgasm. It can also lead to depression, aggression, and a certain lack of joy and sparkle in life.

These symptoms could be due to certain disorders like autism or schizophrenia, but for most of us, low oxytocin comes down purely to one thing: stress. In fact, there is an inverse relationship between the stress hormone cortisol and oxytocin (McQuaid et al., 2016, *Neurobiology of Stress*). When we're stressed, we can disconnect from others—but being disconnected may exacerbate our stress levels, creating a vicious circle.

How can you increase or balance oxytocin in your life?

The good news is that boosting oxytocin is usually free, easy, and enjoyable by definition! Giving birth, breastfeeding, having sex, or being in love release potent doses of oxytocin, but you don't need to have such full-on experiences to add little oxytocin bubbles throughout the day. Any nonsexual contact will do the trick, including hugs, cuddles, holding hands, massages, and eye contact. You can even stimulate oxytocin release by giving yourself a small massage. You can also:

- Give a gift
- Tell someone you love them
- Do yoga or other mind-body exercises
- Listen to music that makes you feel good
- Enjoy a leisurely meal with friends or family
- Try loving kindness meditation
- Have a hot bath
- Play with a pet
- Have a good conversation with someone you care about

One fool-proof way to build more oxytocin in your life is to **consciously create feelings of trust**. Trust encourages oxytocin release. Of course, it's not a good idea to trust someone who is untrustworthy, but if you trust *nobody*, you lose out on opportunities to experience that oxytocin rush. The trick is to start with realistic expectations of others that build trust gradually and surely.

In our world, the default is to be suspicious of others, but commit to courageously taking a risk and sometimes moving out of your comfort zone. Be a little vulnerable with a new friend or trust someone with a new task, even if there is a small risk of disappointment. Sometimes, we can increase feelings of trust simply by not being so quick to judge or condemn—make a deal with yourself that you will delay judgment in ambiguous situations and give everyone the benefit of the doubt in the first instance.

In Stephen Covey's 2006 book, *The Speed of Trust, The One Thing that Changes Everything*, he explains how we also need to commit to being trustworthy people ourselves. Communicate openly and keep your promises—in time, each little engagement and connection will build a trusting network around you. If you deliberately and strategically seek to be generous with your time and trust in others, they will respond in kind. Follow your gut a little more, take time to get to know people, and have a little faith in the good intentions of others.

Finally, stop thinking in terms of transactions and what you can get from people (or what they can get from you!) and think in terms of service, relationships, and interdependence. **Consciously and deliberately cultivating trust** this way navigates a path between too little oxytocin and too much, and finds that sweet spot of connection and contentment.

Serotonin

Serotonin is a powerful mood regulator and plays multiple roles in the body's homeostatic balance, not just as a mood stabilizer, but with nutrient absorption in the gut, immune health, and blood circulation. Serotonin is sometimes called the "confidence molecule" because high levels are associated with lower rejection sensitivity, enabling an individual to place themselves in situations that will increase self-esteem, which in turn means a person deliberately seeks situations that can create feelings of competency and self-esteem.

When serotonin is high, you feel happy, focused, confident, energized, and "in the zone." You don't worry, you're socially engaged, you sleep better, and you overall feel safe and assured in the world. You're resilient. Without serotonin, you're depressed, fearful, and unmotivated. You don't take risks or put yourself "out there" because you lack faith in your own abilities to rise to new challenges or cope with change.

Loretta Breuning is the author of the book *Habits of a Happy Brain* and founder of the Inner Mammal Institute. According to Breuning, "Confidence triggers serotonin. Monkeys try to one-up each other because it stimulates their serotonin. People often do the same." But serotonin also creates feelings of confidence, meaning that it's a catch-22. If you have low self-esteem, it's a sign your serotonin could be low, too. Breuning believes that to maintain healthy levels of serotonin, we need to support our need for respect and status. How?

- **Focus on your wins and achievements**, and don't dwell on failures that can't be changed. Instead, look at how far you've come. Just a few moments of reflecting on your past achievements can give you a boost of serotonin and make you feel proud of yourself.

- As with oxytocin, **challenge yourself** to try something out of your comfort zone now and then. (Soon, we'll see how setting goals can also boost dopamine levels.) Every new challenge is a chance to show yourself *you can do it*, and build feelings of competence.
- **Revisit the way you feel respected**. Your early experiences with what won you respect and esteem established certain neural pathways, but not all of these are healthy or valid. You can respect your need for status while questioning the way you get these needs met. You might have needed to put others down in the past or compete viciously, for example, but what other healthier ways could you feel good about yourself today?
- **Believe in yourself**. This means acknowledging that it's also okay to want some admiration, respect, and acknowledgment for your achievements. Start by giving that to yourself.
- **Exercise**. Research shows that even a little can boost your feelings of confidence and wellbeing.
- **Eat better**. Because most of your body's serotonin is made in the gut, your diet is important. Eat an unprocessed diet rich in fruit and vegetables, wholegrains, and good quality proteins, plus fermented foods and probiotics (such as kimchi, kombucha, or yogurt).
- **Reflect on difficult situations in the past**, but only those that you survived and overcame. This will reaffirm for you that you can do the same in the face of current adversities.
- **Go outside** and get just twenty minutes of natural sunlight on your skin, which has been shown to boost serotonin levels.

- **Connect to your leadership potential**. What do you know and what can you teach others? How can you inspire others with your sense of purpose?
- **Confidently assert boundaries**. Sometimes, confidence looks like being clear and assertive about our limits and needs. Serotonin is created in the gut, so sometimes "trusting your gut" is a way to foster more confidence and self-courage! Simply saying "no" and meaning it can provide a boost of confidence-enhancing serotonin.

Just like with oxytocin, serotonin levels are best balanced consistently and gradually. Don't try to change all at once; rather, find small steps you can take to nurture your sense of self-pride over time. If you find you're being too hard on yourself, pause and remember all the amazing things you've achieved and give yourself permission to feel good about them.

Endorphins

The role of these neurochemicals is to mask pain and make it easier to tolerate discomfort. The word comes from endogenous (meaning "from within") and morphine (a pain-relieving opiate). These natural painkillers are closely connected to the fight-or-flight system and kick in any time we face pain or stress.

However, we also secret endorphins during eating, sex, and exercise (i.e., the famous "runner's high"—the brief euphoria runners experience when they push themselves to their physical limits). In fact, one big reason for exercise being such a consistently prescribed treatment for depression (Dinas et al.,

2010) is that the endorphins it releases act so powerfully to relieve that pain.

It's easy to see why the endorphin mechanism evolved. Pain triggers endorphin release. In the wild, these endorphins help injured or compromised animals ignore pain and continue to avoid predators and seek safety, enhancing their survival. It explains why seemingly exhausted or seriously wounded people are able to act with incredible clarity, strength, and speed in emergency situations . . . and also why certain people get a strange thrill out of self-harming.

High endorphin levels mitigate anxiety and depression, boost self-esteem, modulate appetite, and even enhance immune response. Signs of low endorphin levels include anxiety and depression, mood swings, aches and pains, impulsivity, poor sleep, and even addictions.

How can we increase our endorphin levels? Hopefully, making ourselves feel pain is not the only way!

One obvious way to increase endorphin release is to undertake vigorous exercise—running being the favorite. Any vigorous exercise will do, however, since the tiny tears in the muscle fibers create the mild pain needed to trigger the release of pain-relieving endorphins. However, you can still enjoy more moderate endorphin benefits with two other activities: stretching and laughing.

Both of these slightly disrupt and move your internal organs and create very minor wear and tear that encourages endorphin release (Kumar et al., 2015). The process for a really good-feeling stretch is self-explanatory, and so is laughing—if it's genuine, that is (Manninen et al., 2017, "**Social Laughter**

Triggers Endogenous Opioid Release in Humans"). Eating dark chocolate (Nehlig, 2013, *British Journal of Clinical Pharmacology*, and Magrone et al., 2017), spicy food (Bosland, 2015), watching enjoyable TV shows, or meditating have also shown in various studies to release endorphins.

Verywellmind.com lists a few more surprising possibilities:

- Have sex
- Enjoy or make music
- Enjoy or make art
- Dance
- Try acupuncture
- Get a massage
- Have a nice hot sauna
- Try aromatherapy
- Volunteer
- Spend time with friends

Increased endorphin levels can actually encourage dopamine release (more on this shortly), reminding us that all four of the DOSE neurochemicals interact and work together—just like those cake ingredients!

But there are limits. "Endorphins evolved for survival," says Breuning. "If you were high on endorphins all the time, you would touch hot stoves and walk on broken legs." In other words, remember that endorphins are primarily there for emergency situations, so don't overdo it.

Dopamine

We've left the most interesting neurotransmitter for last. Dopamine is one seriously misunderstood molecule!

In his book *Behave: The Biology of Humans at Our Best and Worst*, Robert M. Sapolsky describes a study that concluded that when a monkey received a reward after pushing a lever, the monkey's brain released dopamine. The next time he pushed the lever, however, his brain released dopamine *before* the reward even appeared, showing that dopamine is not a feeling of satisfaction with a reward, but the pleasant *anticipation* of one.

Sexual arousal, for example, can result in greater dopamine levels than actual sexual fulfilment, just as the act of ordering a delicious meal in a restaurant may feel more emotionally satisfying than taking the first bite! Thus, dopamine is about the expectation of reward and fulfilment and is powerfully connected to reward and a feeling of purpose.

There's a reason this brain chemical evolved. Every time we approach a reward (i.e., something that increases our survival), we trigger dopamine release that basically tells our brains, "This is good! Keep doing this!" So, when a predator is hunting a tasty prey animal, their dopamine levels are through the roof, and this is associated with a system-wide increase in energy levels—energy that is needed to catch the prey.

Dopamine increases a sense of alertness and focus, but the object of that focus can change depending on who you are. Any time we engage in potentially rewarding behavior (eating, having sex, accomplishing a goal), we get a burst of dopamine.

Whenever dopamine flowed when you were young and

in your formative years, certain neural connections in your brain cemented themselves, so you were wired up to seek out those sensations again. Dopamine is a motivation chemical, prompting you to seek out certain behaviors that feel good—and that persistence can take endless forms:

- Scrolling through profile pics on a dating app
- Striving toward a professional qualification
- Chasing that rush you get from winning at gambling
- Figuring out how to finally solve a challenging brain puzzle

In every case, dopamine is there to spur you on to take action toward a goal you are focused on, and it spurs you by making you feel good. A dopamine release is like a little reward along every step of the way, motivating you, encouraging behaviors, and even creating long-term habits (in this case, a habit is: "this felt good in the past, so I will keep doing it in the present").

Dopamine explains why it feels good to have a goal and work to reach it—and it also explains why those with low dopamine can suffer from depression, low motivation, or lack of interest in life.

When it comes to dopamine, then, it is not simply a question of creating more. Rather, it's about *how* you use it and what role it plays in your life. After all, a heroin addict and a highly motivated med student may both have overactive dopamine release, but for very different reasons and with very different results!

How do you optimize your own dopamine levels?

According to Breuning, there are plenty of *unhealthy* ways

to increase dopamine, including overconsumption of caffeine and sugar, and recreational drug use.

But there's one primary healthy way to boost it, and that's to "**embrace a new goal** and take small steps toward it every day. Your brain will reward you with dopamine each time you take a step. The repetition will build a new dopamine pathway until it's big enough to compete with the dopamine habit that you're better off without."

Your goals can be big or small, personal or professional, long term or short term—in fact, it's probably a good idea to mix them up. What matters is being proactive in your goal setting and to take steps toward it—it's these steps that create the sense of dopamine-mediated reward.

A Few Things to Keep in Mind

While the goal itself is important, it's the *little rewards* that lead to it that help cement those dopamine pathways. Break down big tasks into smaller ones and pause to reward yourself often, enjoying your sense of accomplishment and movement. Challenge is good, but don't put the fulfilment of the goal too far off into the future.

If it's difficult to create a feeling of reward, reconnect to your higher purpose behind the goal. This will make you feel that your actions are still connected to the goal, and dopamine will be released. You'll know that you have an issue with dopamine if you feel uninspired, demotivated, bored, or uninterested in life in general. If you notice this happening, it's time to embrace a new goal and ask yourself: what's the first smallest step I can take toward that goal? Notice how you feel after you take that step (hint: probably a lot happier!).

How to Do a Dopamine Detox

When the brain's dopamine reward-system is misaligned or focused on an unhealthy target, it can lead to addictive behavior. With this understanding, there is now a growing trend to partake in "dopamine fasting," a concept first coined by Dr. Cameron Sepah. However, the term can be misleading since the program isn't about fasting at all and creates the misconception that dopamine itself is something harmful that needs to be reduced or eliminated. This is not the case!

Dopamine fasting, Sepah told the *New York Times*, is a behavioral therapy approach that attempts to disconnect from unhealthy stimuli that disrupt our dopamine system, such as push notifications and other digital cues and alarms. The idea is that this constant onslaught of stimuli trains our brains in unhealthy ways; every time our smartphone pings, we get a dopamine burst . . . which cements that neural pathway and has us addictively and compulsively checking our phone, hoping in some way for another "reward."

A dopamine fast, then, is a misnomer since it is not a fast from dopamine, but rather a *re-calibration* exercise. With dopamine fasting, the idea is to regain dopamine sensitivity and find joy in simple, healthy things again. Instead of needing behavior like emotional eating, gambling, excessive porn use and masturbation, novelty seeking, recreational drugs, and addictive gaming, dopamine fasting attempts to reset our habits and untrain our neural pathways. In CBT (cognitive behavioral therapy), this technique is simply known as "stimulus control."

When you experience pleasure (dopamine release) during a behavior, you are more likely to repeat it—the stimulus that triggers the behavior and your response become paired, i.e., the behavior is conditioned. For example, you release dopamine every time you scroll through social media. The stimulus (seeing your phone on the table) now produces a conditioned response (you cannot help but pick up the phone and scroll mindlessly). A dopamine fast is about breaking these conditioned responses—which necessarily means changing your dopamine levels.

If you have noticed any addictive or compulsive behaviors in yourself (given the way that technology is designed, it's almost inevitable), you can do a dopamine fast or "detox." You'll know you have a problem if your habits are getting in the way of your responsibilities and obligations or are causing you distress.

The process is simple . . . but not always easy.

Step 1: Remove the Stimulus

Make the thing that triggers the addictive behavior difficult or impossible to access. You could try to physically remove your smartphone from your presence, install website-blocking tools on your desktop, or schedule certain commitments to coincide with the ties you're most likely to want to engage in the behavior.

If food is a problem, you could make sure to keep forbidden snacks out of the kitchen. If gaming or gambling is the problem, you could make sure that you don't have access to the internet outside of work hours or take a route home that avoids passing by a casino, for example.

Step 2: Practice Urge-Surfing

The impulse to engage in the habit will still arise, because your brain has been wired to expect reward coming from that behavior. Furthermore, it's not always possible to avoid being exposed to the triggering stimulus. So when it does arise, instead of trying to avoid or escape these feelings of craving, try to "sit with" them. "Ride the wave" by merely noticing the urge and realizing that you can experience it without necessarily needing to succumb. Remind yourself that every time you choose not to engage, you weaken that neural pathway.

With a spirit of non-judgment, keep on becoming aware of the impulse, breathe, and *allow it to pass*—because it does! Notice how it increases, reaches a peak, and then dies off again. Each time you do this, you train a different response in yourself. It does get easier.

Step 3: Reconnect to Your Values

In the throes of addiction, it can feel like all you want is to engage in the behavior, and nothing else matters. But this is just proof of how powerfully motivating a chemical like dopamine can be! As you practice Steps 1 and 2, simultaneously see what you can do *instead of* the compulsive behavior. To do this, remind yourself of what you actually value. Is it health, knowledge, connection with loved ones? Chances are, the habit or addictive behavior doesn't ultimately bring you closer to these things, and probably even undermines them.

"Doing nothing" is difficult, if not impossible. But opting instead for a behavior that is aligned with your values will help you normalize your sense of purpose and motivation. Look at all the time in your schedule you save by cutting back on dopamine-spurring behaviors and ask how you can better use that time instead.

Perhaps you can take good care of your health (cook a good meal, exercise, go for a walk), socialize, learn something new, tidy up your home, create or enjoy art, read, listen to music, relax or even sleep, travel, do a hobby, or give back by volunteering.

Remember that dopamine fasting is NOT:

- Trying to live a life of little pleasure (it's about *optimal* levels of dopamine!)
- Trying to reduce dopamine (rather, you are reducing compulsive behavior)
- Being acetic, stopping work, or going on a sabbatical (you are not retreating from life)

Dopamine fasting is more about **balance**. After all, although Internet Addiction is now classified as a psychiatric disorder in the DSM (Diagnostic and Statistical Manual), the clinical consensus (Young, 2015, *Journal of Behavioral Addiction*) is that *moderate and controlled* internet use is preferable to going cold turkey, as it were.

Exactly how you practice dopamine fasting will depend on

you, your "addictions," your goals, and your unique situation. But here are some ideas to get you started:

- Look at your schedule and block out times of day when you won't engage in the behavior, and limited times when you will. For example, you could decide that you only watch TV for an hour on Saturdays and Sundays, no more. Nobody can tell you exactly what *your* limits should be; however, it's important that there are limits.
- Seek balance. Try to moderate your exposure to extreme over-stimulation, such as heavily processed and addictive foods, intense gaming or TV, highly emotive online news content, manipulative advertising, lots of novelties, or thrilling, high-arousal, adrenaline-inducing activities.
- Try not to eliminate behaviors but replace them. You might find that simple distraction at the peak of your craving is enough to divert your attention until more self-control kicks in. For example, install an internet blocking app on your computer and put a book next to it so that you are encouraged to pick it up to entertain yourself instead.

Takeaways:

- Neurotransmitters are the brain's chemical messengers, and there are four major types, called DOSE chemicals, that greatly influence our overall experience: dopamine, oxytocin, serotonin, and endorphins.
- Oxytocin is the love hormone responsible for feelings of

bonding, connection, empathy, and safety. You can increase oxytocin by consciously fostering trust in your social network and being more trustworthy yourself. Think in terms of service, relationships, and interdependence and strategically trust those around you to create warm connections.

- Serotonin is a mood stabilizer and "confidence hormone," which is all about self-esteem, self-determination, and competence. To increase serotonin levels, believe in yourself, confidently assert boundaries, have the courage to lead, and dwell on your achievements rather than your failures.

- Endorphins are the brain's natural painkillers and mitigate anxiety and depression, boost self-esteem, modulate appetite, and even enhance immune response. To increase it, we can try vigorous exercise, spicy foods, stretching, or laughing.

- Dopamine is the brain's reward molecule and involves the anticipation of future pleasure, which cements our habits. We can create more dopamine any time we set a new goal for ourselves and reward ourselves with every baby step toward that goal.

- If you battle with addiction, a dopamine detox or fast might help. Try to avoid or remove the triggering stimulus, but when you inevitably encounter it, practice "urge surfing" and facing discomfort without succumbing. Reconnect to your values to replace the compulsive behavior with something that genuinely brings benefit to your life instead.

3

A BRAINY ROUTINE

Imagine someone who struggles with poor attention and focus, bad self-esteem, and a host of annoying addictive behaviors such as gaming late into the night and drinking a little too much on the weekends. They want to make positive changes to their brain health and start taking much better care of the enormously powerful and magnificent piece of machinery sitting inside their skull.

One day, they buy a "brain boost" supplement that's meant to help with memory, and they take it half-heartedly for a month or so before forgetting about it. Then they play around with a brain-training app on their phone but find it boring and ditch that, too. Knowing a little about neurotransmitters and supporting them for better brain health, they make a plan to be more active, to socialize more, and to commit to value-aligned goals. You already know how it goes: Many of these attempts fizzle out early or never even launch in the first place. Why? What makes it so difficult to take steps to improve your cognitive fitness?

It should be obvious from the research on yoga and dancing that as wonderful as these activities are for body and mind, they are not silver bullets, and their influence lies in our ability to do them *consistently* and harness the power of neuroplasticity and our adaptive brains. It's not a one-off action that makes or breaks the resilience and strength of our brains, but actions over time, i.e., habits, routines, and conscious thought that become unconscious action.

Yoga done weekly for years naturally has a cumulative and more substantial effect than merely dabbling here and there. So does any type of aerobic exercise, we've learned. Making a conscious effort to make your health a priority is what counts—and this is a commitment that can be renewed in every moment of every day, consistently.

Good habits and routines are nothing more than what we all know as common sense—the trick is to actually *do* them! Our health—mental, physical, or emotional—is built on the aggregate of dozens of tiny habits that all may seem insignificant on their own. In the same way, dozens of smaller, poor choices made over and over again soon crystallize into poor health that then takes a lot more effort to shift once in place. Against this crystallized mass, a single half-hearted attempt at health here or there will have very little effect—except perhaps to discourage you and convince you that real change is impossible.

But if you *consistently* maintain yourself mostly within healthy parameters for most of the time, it then becomes almost second nature to stay there. It's a question of momentum—soon, it takes more energy to *not* follow your healthy habit than to break it. It might take a lot of effort to shift old patterns once they've ingrained themselves, but if you can make regular commitments on a small scale, you never put yourself in the position of having to take drastic action to get on the right path again.

It should come as no surprise to anyone that good sleep, exercise, and proper nutrition will all make it significantly easier to maintain your brain in the peak state it needs to be to optimally process the world around you. There are now dozens of different supplements available to boost brain health, and we're all aware of the different foods that are meant to "feed your brain." One aspect that even health-conscious people tend to forget, however, is perhaps the most important one: proper rest and sleep. It's the first cornerstone of a set of daily routines and habits to keep you at your peak mental performance.

Hello, Mr. Sandman

It seems both obvious and an understatement, and yet, we don't treat sleep with the respect and reverence it deserves.

It's no exaggeration to say that our world is rushed. We favor action, results, ego-driven goals, and the relentless pursuit of them, whether our bodies can keep up or not. With so much talk of boosting productivity, of "hustle" culture, of no pain and no gain, one could understandably think we all want to turn ourselves into robots that work twenty-four-seven and never indulge in something so unproductive as . . . taking naps.

The bitter irony is that, as so many burnt-out businesspeople inevitably learn, rest does not distract or take away from our active success, but is integral to it. Those who can't rest are often forced to slow down when their bodies simply pack it in. Without mentioning all the physical harm it does to run the body ragged and ignore signals to relax and recoup, it's also obvious that sleeping poorly is terrible for our mental and intellectual health. In our culture, rest and sleep are seen as weaknesses instead of rightfully considered as an integral part of the hustle process. Somehow it seems more difficult to connect because the brain only sends subtle signals of mental exhaustion, such as reading the same paragraph over and over, in lieu of a muscle cramp in your calf.

Sleep is not optional. It's a biological need as paramount as air, water, and food. Though it's true that scientists are only just beginning to understand *why* we sleep at all, it's one hundred percent certain that we cannot function without it. In 2013, research by Bjorn Rasch and colleagues showed us that sleep is vital for maintaining how our brains learn and store new information as memories. It's as though in sleep, the brain reviews and replays what new information it encountered during the day, and solidifies it into memories that are then more easily retrieved when necessary.

You might have even noticed this for yourself—that a poor night's sleep has you feeling a little slower than normal, perhaps forgetting things you might have otherwise remembered. There is an old urban legend that going without sleep can make you literally crazy, but it turns out that lack of sleep really can produce hallucinations and acute psychotic states. Prolonged periods of sleep deprivation, however, are associated with even more serious disorders like Alzheimer's, as found in 2018 in a National Institutes of Health study. This is because a lack of sleep eventually exacerbates the creation of misshapen proteins that aggregate in the brain and form plaques, inhibiting the normal function of your neurons.

Other than using the sleep state to consolidate learning, the brain also needs to rest deeply so that it can properly dispose of wastes accumulated throughout the day. These "housekeeping" activities are performed while you sleep and account for that refreshed feeling you get when you wake up after a really good rest. The glymphatic system is a network of vessels that drain cerebrospinal fluid from the brain along with the brain's metabolic waste. The system works best at night; when you don't sleep, you don't give your brain the chance to tidy up.

All those misshapen proteins that would otherwise form plaques in the brain? These are regularly cleared away by the glymphatic system. As we age, the accumulation of these wonky proteins increases, possibly leading to neurodegenerative diseases. It's not a metaphor to say that those with Alzheimer's or Parkinson's disease have tangled brains—these misshapen proteins act as literal knots that clump around the neurons and impair their function, hence a range of symptoms like memory loss, motor defects, and even mood disruptions.

When you sleep poorly, what would have been cleared away by the glymphatic system is left to accumulate in the brain, eventually reaching toxic levels if sleep deprivation is chronic. Worse still is that simply being in a sleep-deprived state can in turn make it more difficult to sleep. Bad sleep habits tend to breed more bad sleep habits, setting up a vicious circle that's harder and harder to escape from.

These effects can be noted even with a single night's poor

sleep. This is normal and happens to us all, and there is nothing to worry about if you soon catch up, giving your body the chance to re-balance itself. But consistent poor-quality sleep can impact your cognitive performance, your mood, and even your immune system in ways that may not be all that reversible.

A 2009 study by Gujar et al. even showed that lack of sleep disrupts emotions and the brain's reward systems. Essentially, the researchers found that being sleep deprived makes people more sensitive to "rewarding" stimuli, to which they react with heightened emotional response. This could lead to addictive or repetitive behaviors, irrational behavior, or the symptoms we typically associate with mood disorders.

Ehsan Shokri-Kojori of the National Institutes of Health and his colleagues found that one night of bad sleep increased protein aggregation in the brain by around five percent in the right hippocampus and thalamus. Such an accumulation may lead to a grumpy mood the next day, but will in all likelihood be cleared away the next night—if you sleep well, that is.

Can we ever clear ourselves completely of this sleep debt that appears to have such negative consequences? It can take weeks to months, and sleep expert Elena Winnel suggests that we can only really catch up on about twenty hours of debt, so if we continue to sacrifice sleep, we put our brains in a semi-permanent compromised state.

Oh, and sleep debt also reduces insulin sensitivity, which leads to fat retention, weight gain, poor blood sugar regulation, and the increased risk of diabetes and obesity.

What used to be a relatively unexplored area in medicine is now being more fully appreciated as an integral part of health and wellness. There's no getting around it: sleep is a pillar of a healthy life, not just for the brain but the entire body. Improving sleep is not just about reducing your risk of serious disease, but about making sure you're giving yourself the best chance to succeed every day. A good mood, a brain that works, and a sufficient level of energy are the bare minimum to keep doing your best in *any* endeavor.

So, forget productivity apps or weird tips and tricks designed to squeeze more out of your brain. In fact, you can probably find vast stores of untapped energy and potential simply by sleeping better, rather than opting for supplements, tools, tricks, and hacks that can do nothing anyway if your body is too exhausted to make use of them. You can support yourself best by simply pulling back when you're tired and giving your brain the time it needs to recuperate. Sacrifice some sneaky and subtle tactics for an additional hour of sleep, and you'll perform far better.

Practice good sleep hygiene with the same care as you would give your diet or exercise regime. This means regular times to sleep and wake, getting at least eight hours quality sleep, and making sure your room is free of distracting sounds and lights as you're sleeping or preparing for bed. Invest in a good mattress, comfortable bedding, and breathable pajamas.

Make sure that every day, without fail, you give yourself a few minutes every evening for a bedtime ritual so you can wind down and allow your brain to relax from a busy day. Meditation, yoga, a warm bath, gentle reading, doodling (more on this later), quiet music, or relaxed conversation will all help you slow down so you can get the best out of your night's sleep.

One final component of great sleep hygiene is to regularly take naps. In our work-obsessed culture, you may feel a little guilty for taking an hour-long nap during the day, since you feel you'd be "wasting time." But it may help to reframe daytime napping as intelligent self-care, as a regular health practice, or even, on some days in particular, an emergency measure! Have you ever found yourself in a truly atrocious mood, only to cheer up after a good long nap? There was likely nothing better you could have done for your mood than simply step back and disengage for a moment.

Think about the culture surrounding the midday "siesta" (Spanish for *sleep*) in many cultures, including Spanish, Italian, and even some Asian countries. People of these cultures noticed that relaxing, with or without sleep, tended to help productivity and increase happiness of workers, at the very least. Sometimes, deliberately not focusing on a task at hand or a problem you're trying to solve can make it easier to crack when you return to it after a complete break. When you switch tasks or do "nothing," you are actually giving your brain the opportunity to process without further demands, and certain unconscious mechanisms can often kick in, leaving you with insights and solutions that you seemed to arrive at without effort.

Junxin Li and colleagues found in their 2016 research that those adults who had a moderate nap in the daytime surprisingly showed a boost in cognitive performance compared to those who napped for less than thirty minutes or more than ninety minutes—or not at all. And theirs is not the only study to show this. Many other researchers have found that napping enhances subsequent problem-solving ability, promotes better creative thinking, and gives you a sharper memory. In the same way that a good night's sleep can leave you feeling bright-eyed and ready to take on the world, a midday nap can give your brain the little rest it needs to perform well for the rest of the day. A strategic nap can feel like a much-needed "reset," especially if you've been working hard.

However, this comes with an important caveat: Try to ensure that your naps are not interfering with your nighttime sleep routine. Do this by napping for moderate amounts of time only, and avoid napping too early or too late in the day—after lunch is ideal. Find a cool, dark room, close your eyes, and empty your mind. Noises or distractions could only wind up having the opposite effect than you're looking for, so set aside your phone and put anxieties to the side for a while—you can always return to them in an hour. If you find that you're having difficulty falling asleep every night, try shortening your daytime naps or taking one only every other day. You might also find it useful to nap at different times in the day—avoid scheduling a nap too soon after waking in the morning or too close to bedtime.

Take the opportunity during naptime to not just sleep but indulge in a little window of relaxation and escape during the day. Far from being lazy, this allows you to gather your thoughts, process emotions, calm down physiologically as well as mentally, and enjoy some alone time. You don't need a lot of time for it to feel like a luxurious treat and a moment of self-care rolled all in one. Do a little breathing exercise, spend some time meditating or visualizing, or simply contemplate the sounds of birds or cars outside. Relax your muscles and breathe.

Life and all its bustle and noise will be ready for you when you wake up again, but your brain will be in a much better state to tackle it all.

The Power of Mother Earth

Nature is a surprising force multiplier. It has the ability to improve our mental faculties and well-being without us even noticing it. It's probably no coincidence, and we have evolved to seek out greener pastures, sunnier fields, healthier vegetation, and so on. Numerous studies have demonstrated the mental impact of surrounding yourself with elements of nature.

This doesn't mean that if you work in an office or have a similar indoor job, you need to resign immediately and move to a forest. It doesn't matter where you are, but what you can do to take advantage of the world around you—you can easily make it part of your daily routine, as per this chapter's theme. There are several quick and easy things you can change in your daily environment so that you are closer to nature and taking advantage of all the benefits the natural world can provide.

Nature can be calming, soothing, inspiring, and grounding, and it also helps you focus and remember better. More specifically, just staring at an image merely *associated* with nature has been found to improve your working mindset. The *Journal of Environmental Psychology* published a study by University of Melbourne's Kate Lee and a group of colleagues about the power of looking at green.

The experiment asked participants to engage in a long and tedious activity that required complete concentration and a high attention to detail for a long time.

At the midway point, half the participants took a forty-second break and looked at an image of a green rooftop covered with vegetation, while the other half looked at an image of a concrete rooftop. The study found that interrupting a tedious, attention-demanding task with the green rooftop dramatically improved focus and resulted in better overall performance on their task.

The participants reported that it felt more restorative, and they performed especially well in their response times, lessened their fluctuation in reactions, and made fewer errors of omission.

This is one of the easiest things to implement in a busy daily routine. Hanging a painting, sticking up a poster, or even just searching the Internet will do the trick. A picture or computer background will suffice. Even better, set an alarm and go for a quick walk outside and see nature up close if you can. A quick forty-second look, and you'll be ready to return to any task.

Is this phenomenon because something in us subconsciously recognizes the primacy of nature? Is green an innately soothing color because it's what we were surrounded by for millennia? Is there really something to the calming power of nature? It seems so, and the next few studies continue to show the same trend.

Harsh lighting and artificial light are everywhere. Long gone are the days where we woke with the sun and slept when it set. In today's modern world, we're always trying to fit in as much work as we can, and we're not always in the best atmosphere to do so. Several studies prove working in natural light is beneficial to our mental well-being and happiness.

The Neuroscience Program at Northwestern University

showed a strong relationship between workplace daylight exposure and office workers' sleep, activity, and quality of life.

According to the study, employees slept forty-six minutes more per night on average if they worked in natural light. They also slept more soundly and efficiently and reported a higher quality of life than those who did not work in natural light. Workers in windowless environments had lower scores in their physical health and vitality than those who worked near daylight. They also reported poorer sleep quality, with sleep disturbances and daytime dysfunction.

Natural light has many health-related benefits and can feel mentally more satisfying as well. A lack of natural light has been documented to disrupt the body's circadian rhythms, which are behavioral changes that respond to light and darkness in one's environment. By disturbing our circadian rhythms, a lack of natural light can cause abnormal sleep patterns and also seasonal affective disorder, which results in multiple symptoms such as depression and lethargy.

All of this means that without natural light, your body will be significantly less productive and energized. If you can, try to change your work environment so that you are exposed to natural light as much as possible. If this is impossible, like if you work in a windowless office, you can buy lamps that simulate natural light.

A study in Britain, published in *The Responsible Workplace*, also supported the importance of natural light. The study showed that of the many factors that influenced the occupants' level of satisfaction with a building, windows were the number-one determinant. Natural light renovations have been shown to result in happy workers and a better overall work environment, with less absenteeism and fewer illnesses. Furthermore, because of worker satisfaction from the better lighting, the employees also increased their productivity.

In a final study on natural light, Christopher Jung of the University of Colorado showed that natural light can reduce our level of cortisol, which means we will feel less stressed under natural light conditions. Natural light literally calms us down on a biological and hormonal level.

With all of these benefits of natural light, it seems foolish to prevent ourselves from being exposed to it as often as we can. So stop working like a hermit and open your windows to the sun. If you can't do this, find a way to be exposed to natural light, with a lamp that simulates it if you really have to. Take a walk on your lunch break, sit by a window when you can, or take your work elsewhere. Find a way to bask in the sun's rays and you'll feel all the better for it. Just wear sunscreen from time to time.

On a related note, the more you learn about plants, the more you realize that they will always have additional benefits. If you are someone who likes to have plants or vegetation around, even if it's just because you think they're pretty or you needed a simple way to decorate, you're already one step ahead of the game.

Several studies have proven the benefits of working with plants around you, even if it's just that small shrub in the corner. One of these studies demonstrated that employees randomly assigned to work in a room filled with plants outperformed those who didn't have access to plants.

Another study, conducted in the UK and the Netherlands by Marlon Nieuwenhuis from Cardiff University's School of Psychology, addressed employee perception of plants. When office workers could see a plant from their desks, their perceptions of air quality, concentration, and workplace satisfaction and their objective measures of productivity all increased.

So why are plants so beneficial for our mental well-being and performance? We are all aware of the oxygen-providing attribute of plants, but they are also able to suck carbon dioxide and other relatively benign toxins from the air. This is why the workers perceived cleaner and more concentrated air in their offices—whether it was true or not. But plants also appear to provide a considerable overall calming effect, and they've been known to reduce levels of stress. This is perfect for stressful environments like your work. In addition, plants can help absorb noise, and quiet is often essential for a working environment.

It's not entirely clear just why plants can have such a positive impact on us mentally. Perhaps it's just subconscious, or a way to take us out of a stressful work environment by reminding us what's outside or waiting for us when we are finished. Perhaps it's the placebo effect taking hold thanks to the supposedly fresher air we are sucking in. Regardless, the evidence is undeniable and, again, easy to implement as part of a daily routine.

A final demonstration of the power of nature lies in research regarding the most popular pictures and videos on the Internet. At last, after all those hours spent staring at adorable newborn pandas or sleeping kittens, the research is finally here to back you up. Maybe that urge to look at cute pictures of baby animals isn't as unproductive as you once thought. You can finally let go of the guilt you've been harboring for "wasting time."

A Japanese research paper appropriately titled "The Power of Kawaii: Viewing Cute Images Promotes a Careful Behavior and Narrows Attentional Focus" concluded that looking at cute animal images at work could boost your focus, attention to detail, and overall performance on a task. The study, conducted by Hiroshi Nottono of the University of Hiroshima, studied three different groups of students as they performed several tasks. These ranged from visual tasks to those involving dexterity, with one being similar to the American board game Operation. Each group attempted its respective activity twice—the first time without looking at any images, and the second time after looking at a series of pictures. These images could have included baby animals, adult animals, or neutral subjects such as foods.

Students who viewed cute animal pictures performed far better at their tasks than their peers who saw pictures of adult animals or food. There are many theorized explanations linked to this improvement.

One suggested reason was related to a behavioral tendency in humans to slow down their speech when talking to babies, puppies, and kittens. Researchers speculated that looking at images of baby animals might have had a similar effect in slowing not just speech but the behavior of the students. As such, they were more careful and attentive during their tasks and performed more accurately than their peers.

Another offered explanation was to do with nurturing instincts that may have been brought up when looking at the young animals. The researchers suspected that perhaps those who received an increase in nurturing feelings might have performed better in care-related tasks that aimed to help someone, even if it was only in the form of a board game.

Whatever the reason, the study determined that the simple act of looking at the photos was enough to increase focus and attention when they were viewed before a task. It stated that "if viewing cute things makes the viewer more attentive, the performance of a non-motor perceptual task would also be improved."

So if you've been secretly viewing these cute pictures at your desk in the office, trying to hide the fact that you may be doing something unproductive, next time, just go ahead. Chances are you could be boosting your productivity without even knowing it.

The world around us can be far more helpful to boosting our brains than we realize. Nature is all around us and is so easily accessible that it would be a complete waste not to take advantage of everything it can give us. Ultimately, the why is not so important as it is to simply realize the benefits.

Mechanical Actions

Two more practices you can implement into your daily routines are mechanical actions: repetitive behaviors you perform with your body that act to help your focus and thinking.

First, we come to *doodling*. Yes, doodling—the small scribbles or masterpieces you create in your notebooks or the tiny stick figures you draw in the margins. Apparently doodling isn't as undesirable as we were once told in school.

A psychologist from the University of Plymouth, Jackie Andrade, performed a study to test whether doodling really did have an effect on memory and focus. The participants all listened to a monotonous recording, and half of them were asked to doodle while the other half were not. When asked to recall the information they'd just listened to, the doodlers demonstrated significantly higher recall than the non-doodlers.

It may seem that doodling would only serve as a distraction, as it might draw your attention onto whatever you're drawing rather than the task you should be focusing on. However, Andrade argues against this: "People may doodle as a strategy to help themselves concentrate . . . We might not be aware that we're doing it, but it could be a trick that people develop because it helps them from wandering off into a daydream."

This suggests that instead of distracting you and pulling you away from the task, doodling might just be grounding your thoughts with a subconscious activity that requires minimal concentration, while the rest of you absorbs information.

The scientists hypothesized that unlike daydreaming, which involves a significantly larger mental demand, the mental load required to doodle is quite small and doesn't lead your mind entirely astray from the task you are supposed to be engaged in. The small iota of your attention that is preoccupied with doodling actually appears to keep you focused and centered in the present time, giving you a release valve from the frustrations of an overly long or tiresome task.

This might also be due to the fact that we are very visual people; our entire world is centered on what we can see. A whopping thirty percent of our brains are devoted to processing visual information. While you're being bombarded with information, a visual task such as doodling can help you form associations and therefore process things much better.

American author Sunni Brown is known for extolling the power of doodling. According to her research, doodling can help you "anchor a task." This means it will keep you focused during a long meeting or phone call. Concentrate on scribbling pictures or designs that reflect what you're hearing or thinking. It doesn't matter if they are funny or weird or have nothing to do with what you are discussing. Doodling will help keep your thoughts from straying, and you might be surprised at how much you will be able to recall of a conversation afterward.

If doodling won't work for you, then use the general idea of visual stimuli to help you. When you need to brainstorm ideas, try a pen and paper diagram with as many visual representations as you can come up with. When you have a lot to do, write a physical to-do list and place it somewhere easily accessible so you will always have it in sight. Or even leave a notebook and pen beside you so that when you hit a stopping point in your work, you can try to reason it out visually. The point is that a visual model may help you organize and focus your thoughts so that you can reach ideas or methods of action.

The second mechanical action is … chewing gum.

How can something as easy as chewing gum help you improve your focus? Well, research conducted by the *British Journal of Psychology* shows that chewing gum increases the oxygen flow to certain parts of your brain that are responsible for your attention span—the prefrontal cortex, which resides over what are generally known as *executive functions*. This extra oxygen means that you will be more alert, and your reflexes will improve as well.

Seems too good to be true? Wait, there's more. The increased blood flow also improves your long-term memory so you are able to store and recall more information. This is very helpful when you are trying to study or learn material for work, or if you need to remember specific protocols. Gum also injects a little bit of insulin into your blood. This little shot of insulin gives you an added energy boost, reinvigorating your brain and motivating you to get out of that slump you may find yourself in.

So gum is actually a truly effective booster of mental performance. Best of all, unlike many other mental performance enhancers, gum itself is responsible for all sorts of benefits without any side effects. The latest investigation into gum for brain health is from a team of psychologists at St. Lawrence University. They conducted an experiment to see the effect of gum on the brain and whether it actually did help to improve performance.

The experiment went like this: 159 students were presented with a number of very demanding cognitive tasks, such as repeating random numbers backward and solving challenging logic puzzles. Half of the subjects chewed gum (sugar-free and sugar-added), while the other half didn't chew anything.

Here's where things got interesting. The subjects who were randomly assigned to chew gum significantly outperformed the others in five out of six of the tests. The only exception was in the sixth test, which was in verbal fluency, where subjects needed to name as many words as possible from a given category, such as "animals." The gum's sugar content had no effect on the performance.

Even though it seems hard to believe, gum might just be the answer to your struggling work cycle. It's a cheap and easy method to try to give you the added push to get you sucked back into your work. If you're not a gum fan, you can still use this research to help you. Gum increases attention span because it increases oxygen flow to the brain. You can replicate this by taking short exercise breaks through your day—even just five minutes to tackle some stairs and you will be more alert. If you can't exercise, sometimes taking a break to breathe very deeply for a moment or two can be more than helpful.

They improve not only your attention span, but also your memory. That's not to say you'll immediately be able to finish that mountain of work you've been avoiding for far too long, but gum may just be a quick way to help get you back on track and focused once more.

Thinking About Thankfulness

We associate the emotion of gratitude with thankfulness for whatever comes into our lives, positive or not. Although the adage of being grateful for what we have is well-known, it's not always a practice we grasp, even though there's *always* something to be grateful for. Still, studies have shown that just being aware of or questioning your gratitude—even if you can't think of anything to appreciate off the top of your head—can create some powerful chemical changes.

For example, stop reading for a minute and consider

five things you're grateful for. They don't need to be big accomplishments or achievements; they can be simple parts of everyday living. "I have clean air to breathe," "I have family and friends who love me," "I have a place to sleep," "I live in interesting times."

Now compare this to the everyday life of someone in abject poverty who's struggling to make ends meet and is on the brink of starvation. Or consider the tale of a ballet dancer who had to have her feet amputated (or something similarly morbid and unfortunate).

You might not have noticed any immediate changes, but a slight feeling of acceptance and perspective probably just entered your mind. You may not have everything that you want (none of us ever do), but your life is still pretty darn good. And it's been scientifically proven that gratitude is more or less a natural antidepressant.

Thinking about or asking what you're grateful for activates certain neural circuits that produce dopamine and serotonin, the neurotransmitters that regulate our pleasure centers and mood levels. They then travel the neural pathways to the "bliss" center of the brain, much like a prescribed antidepressant. The more you stimulate these neural pathways, the stronger and more automatic they become, and the more your resilience and calm become a natural way of living.

Hebb's law states, "Neurons that fire together wire together." We see this proverb at work in everyday life. When you're walking through a forest for the first time, you're forging a new path that can provide challenges. But the more you travel that path, the more defined and easier to follow it becomes.

So it works with the human brain. The more a neural pathway is activated, the less effort it takes to animate it the next time. Since the practice of mental gratitude greases the neurons, simple, short daily meditations on your appreciation can actually ease your tension on a biological level.

Researchers Robert A. Emmons and Michael E. McCullough performed a study in 2003 called "Counting Blessings Versus Burdens: An Experimental Investigation of Gratitude and Subjective Well-Being in Daily Life." They gathered a group of young adults and told them to keep journals. One group was instructed to write daily entries of things they were grateful for, and the other was told to write about their annoyances or why they were better off than other people.

The researchers' instructions to the gratitude journalists encouraged them to note any facet of their lives they were grateful for, regardless of importance: "There are many things in our lives, both large and small, that we might be grateful about. Think back over the past week and write down on the lines below up to five things in your life that you are grateful or thankful for."

For journalists who were given the task of writing down their annoyances, the researchers said: "Hassles are irritants—things that annoy or bother you. They occur in various domains of life, including relationships, work, school, housing, finances, health, and so forth. Think back over today and, on the lines below, list up to five hassles that occurred in your life."

The results were predictably persuasive. The gratitude journalists showed greater increases in determination, attention, enthusiasm, and energy. Their findings showed gratitude to be a powerful social and spiritual accelerator:

> The experience of gratitude, and the actions stimulated by it, build and strengthen social bonds and friendships. Moreover, encouraging people to focus on the benefits they have received from others leads them to feel loved and cared for by others . . . Therefore, gratitude appears to build friendships and other social bonds. These are social resources because, in times of need, these social bonds are wellsprings to be tapped for the provision of social support. Gratitude, thus, is a form of love, a consequence of an already formed attachment as well as a precipitating condition for the formation of new affectional bonds . . . Gratitude is also likely to build and strengthen a sense of spirituality, given the strong historical association between gratitude and religion... Finally, to the extent that gratitude, like other positive emotions, broadens the scope of cognition and enables flexible and creative thinking, it also facilitates coping with stress and adversity.

Just as tellingly, the study proved that realizing that other people are worse off does *not* equal gratitude. Rather, gratitude is an appreciation of the positive aspects of your own situation. Emmons and McCullough's findings could inspire you to try journaling yourself. Putting your thoughts in writing is almost always a good practice.

Start out by writing down five things that you're grateful for. Make a conscious effort to reflect upon the things that bring you joy, elation, or peace of mind. As we've said, there's *always* something to be thankful for in a given situation. It might bring you additional perspective to write five things you have that most people do *not* have. Sometimes it's only through contrast that we can truly keep gratitude in mind.

Commit to this practice every day for the next ten days. Keep a journal by your bed and take a minute before sleeping to recall the events of the day that made you smile. Or start a list on your smartphone to write pleasant events down as they happen (also a quick pick-me-up when you're not having a great day). You can also find an "accountability partner" to keep a list like yours. Every week, you can check in for five minutes and read your lists to each other.

This practice can turn gratitude into your own mental gym—strength training for your neural pathways. The more you practice the act of gratitude, the healthier that muscle gets. Just like in physical gyms, the more you show up and work the gratitude angle, the easier the workouts get.

We get used to whatever situations surround us without much effort. Initiating gratitude in all walks of our own lives might be a more trying task or even impractical in certain situations. When was the last time you turned the key in your car's ignition and praised the miracles of the internal combustion engine? Have you ever taken a walk through a city park and expressed thanks for arch supports? Do you take time from work to appreciate the craft and convenience of your hole punch or stapler?

The central point is that gratitude is simple to execute but not always easy to maintain. There's nothing wrong about expressing annoyances over little inconveniences, but letting those irritations inform the core of our beings is ill-advised.

We've seen how our brain transforms itself based on even our smallest impulses. If we can make gratitude a more constant and consistent impulse, our brains will see to it that our happiness improves.

Takeaways:

- For our purposes, a daily routine is simply a set of actions you can implement to consistently improve your brain health and mental performance. Taken together, these are all helpful for your mental hygiene, and even more so when they become your unconscious habits and natural pattern of behavior.

- We must start with a good night's sleep, as it is the basis for everything. Without sleep, there is no energy, and there is nothing else your brain can devote attention to. Sleep, and even frequent napping, is a force multiplier; this means that it alone is an enormous catalyst to either improve your daily mental performance or flush it down the toilet. Give it the respect it deserves; it's not only about your energy levels, but there are very real neurological changes in the face of sleep debt.

- Surprisingly (or not), nature alone has great power. And this is not in the sense that natural disasters such as hurricanes and earthquakes can alter our lives. There is tremendous influence in simply seeing green foliage, exposing yourself to natural light, having plants in your workspace, and even looking at pictures or videos of animals. The exact mechanism by which this helps us is not known, but it is theorized that nature simply grounds us and reduces our stress to a place where we can focus better. It causes us to be more mindful and aware of our surroundings, mood, and place in the world.

- Some simple actions can also work in the same way to concentrate our efforts and ground us. Chewing gum and doodling while you are thinking or speaking has been shown to improve memory and focus.

- Finally, the practice of daily gratitude has been shown to increase happiness, focus, and even energy. Unlike the other elements of daily routines in this chapter, gratitude consciously grounds you and makes you think about your actions more intentionally, and there are real hormonal and biological changes as a result.

4

THE SOCIAL BRAIN

The health of your brain and mind is, as we've seen, intimately bound up with the health of your body. But that's not all. Your brain is a marvelous organ with the sole purpose of making sense of the world around you—and that world includes other people. No (wo)man is an island, as they say, and a corollary is that no (wo)man's mental health is completely isolated from the quality of his or her interactions with others.

Relationships are at the foundation of good mental health, with many psychologists now understanding that loneliness, depression, and heartbreak can be just as debilitating as more "serious" diseases like diabetes or hypertension. Humans are social animals, and so much of our identity, our sense of fulfillment, our joy, and our purpose in life comes directly from our connection with others. Whether that's family, friends, or the community at large, mental and cognitive health is about not just solid neural connections in the brain, but social, familial, and romantic connections with others. You might even argue that it's an evolutionary quirk that sex, socialization, and being around others helped us be healthier and increase our chances of survival.

Getting It On

In fact, for a specific example, there are now several different pieces of research that show a robust connection between regular sex and better cognitive health. A 2010 study showed that sexual activity was linked with neurogenesis (that is, brain growth) in male rats, and a 2013 study found that daily sexual activity also improved overall cognitive function in rats. You might suppose that rats are just primal beasts that function on only a limited set of drives, but in reality, humans are not so different.

So what about studies involving humans? A more recent 2016 study of more than seven thousand older adults showed they performed much better on cognitive tests when they had engaged in any kind of sex within the previous year than their counterparts who had not. Similar studies have also shown that sexual activity has a definite relationship with memory, improving long-term memory recall.

How this finding relates to younger people or those without memory impairment is up for debate. And, crucially, memory performance still declined in older people, whether they had sex or not, suggesting that sex doesn't prevent memory loss with age. However, the research tells us that our *baseline* memory capacity may be improved by having a more active sex life, which means cognitive decline in later years may seem less pronounced.

While research like this is certainly interesting, it probably paints a very two-dimensional picture of a much more complicated phenomenon. These studies controlled for some factors and found that more emotionally fulfilling sexual experiences tended to yield a greater cognitive benefit. If you remember what we learned about oxytocin and its powerful effect on the brain, this probably won't come as a surprise.

Research studies like these suggest it's not the physical event of sex alone that is good for brain health, but the broader meaning such encounters have for the people involved. It's obvious that those who are in healthy, loving, mutually fulfilling relationships will derive more from sex, and in turn enjoy more of the cognitive benefits. We'll get to that soon.

Again, it pays to remember that correlation is not causation, and we still don't understand if there is perhaps a third variable that independently causes both better cognitive health *and* more regular sex. Perhaps better sex lives and better brain health come from a third variable, a relatively stress-free life? We also don't know the frequency of sex that would be ideal for peak brain health, as it's likely to be different for different people. What we do know, however, is that feeling loved by a supportive partner can act as a powerful protectant against both physical and mental disorders of all kinds.

It's one thing to practice better sleep hygiene or make sure you're getting enough exercise, but this aspect of personal development is perhaps a little more nuanced. It's probably a tad more complicated than "have more sex," but it's also not an exaggeration to say that your sex life is a vital part of your general well-being and deserves your consideration and care—if it's not already up to scratch, that is. If you have a partner, focus on increasing not merely the frequency of sex but the quality. Whatever the physical or cognitive benefits of sex are, a deeply meaningful, loving, satisfying encounter is likely better for you than getting the job done simply in the vague hope that it's good for you!

Again, we find that it's impossible to avoid the holistic nature of human health. If you're having difficulties in your relationship, therapy, better communication, or taking the time to enjoy one another again can have immense benefits. This can directly improve your sex life, strengthening the relationship and boosting your overall sense of belonging and connection in the world. Over and above the endorphin rush and moderate cardio an occasional romp may give you, you're also giving yourself the chance to connect in the most profound of ways with another human being, and perhaps get a little confidence boost too.

There are no studies to corroborate this yet, but the romantic in all of us would like to believe that those ecstatic moments shared between lovers are not just recreational, but deeply enriching to us on many levels. In the same way you can lose yourself in dance or become engrossed in nature or a meditative practice, you can melt into the ego-less moment of bliss that is orgasm and forget about your troubles, your limitations, your fears and doubts. In the process, you strengthen your connection with a loved one and remember that life is, at a fundamental level, meant to be relished and enjoyed, to be shared and experienced with another. What could be more energizing and healthful than that?

Again, though, as far as brain-boosting advice goes, this one is a little tricky. If you're in a relationship already, the research is clear: Do your best to nurture a happy, regular sex life. If not, however, that doesn't mean that you can't reap the cognitive benefits some other way. While sex is marvelous, perhaps it's the *emotional* bond that is most valuable—a bond that can be found with friends, family, or colleagues.

Perhaps you're wondering—what about pornography or masturbation? There is now mounting and alarming evidence that pornography is extremely detrimental not just to the physical health of the brain, but to mental health in general, not to mention potential damage to real-life relationships.

A 2019 article in *Neuroscientist News* put it plainly: Pornography use can erode the prefrontal cortex (the part of the brain responsible for critical thinking and impulse control), interfere with the brain's dopamine systems, and even "rewire the brain to a more juvenile state."

The consequences are neurochemical, physical, behavioral, and some would argue social and even spiritual. Psychiatrist Norman Doige, who treats those with porn-induced sexual dysfunction, puts it this way:

> "Pornography satisfies every one of the prerequisites for neuroplastic change. When pornographers boast that they are pushing the envelope by introducing new, harder themes, what they don't say is that they must, because their customers are building up a tolerance to the content."

Porn addiction has been connected to sexual violence, impaired moral development, depression, relationship breakdown, and the destruction of the cognitive mechanisms that support natural and healthy relationships with real human beings, such as the mirror neuron system (Iacoboni, 2013), empathy, and both oxytocin and dopamine balance (Weaver et al., 2011). One study found that three hours a week was enough to create measurable reductions in gray matter (Kuhn, Gallant, 2014).

The science is clear: Loving and healthy sex is good for the human brain; pornography isn't.

We Were Meant to Mingle

Scientists discovered long ago that social animals have different (and bigger!) brains than animals that are solitary. In mammals especially, brain size correlates with complexity of social interaction. The reason is obvious: to understand another's motivations, to develop language, to engage with others, to fight, to flirt, to gossip, to remember names, to negotiate—all of this takes considerable brain power. It goes the other way too: When a social animal like a human being is lonely or alienated, he suffers not just mentally but physically. We evolved in a complex, social world of small groups, and to this day, we function better when we have friends, romantic partners, and family members to share life with.

Our brains are designed to connect with others. Having a healthy social life is like an immune system, only one that is external to your body. Besides the obvious benefits of having someone to help you through troubles, bounce ideas off of, or simply have a good time with, friends boost our sense of community and belonging. They add immense value and color to life.

Psychologists will frequently enquire about a patient's support network because they know that solid social connections are strongly associated with better outcomes and more stable mental health. In 2007, Oscar Yberra found that when he studied the social habits of 3600 people, those who socialized more had better cognitive performance overall. If you're intending to improve your cognitive function and make the best of your brain, it's clear: you can't do it alone. It might seem like a good idea to pick up a Sudoku puzzle or read to feed your brain, but the happy truth is that you can support your brain health by simply calling up a friend for a chat.

Loneliness and isolation are dangerous—and not just because they feel bad. Low mood, feelings of alienation, and disconnection are all powerful precursors to depression and anxiety, not to mention they encourage unhealthy or addictive coping behaviors that come along with them. For older people especially, retiring from work and retreating from social activity can seriously put cognitive health at risk. In a 2008 study by Crooks and colleagues, older women were shown to have reduced risk of dementia with age if they were a part of large social groups. Conversely, those who are bereaved, battling chronic illness, or are merely alone will find the natural course of aging accelerated and neurodegenerative disease setting in earlier.

Crucially, however, it's worth defining what "social interaction" really is. Unfortunately, many of us have grown up in a digital world, where our social lives have shifted online and become decidedly more unreal. With a wave of new research showing that social media use is often linked to worse mental health, it's important to realize that nothing can replace *genuine* interaction with people you care about, preferably in person. Natural, real-time conversation and the ability to engage with a person directly is always going to be more satisfying than sitting in front of a pixelated screen, looking at curated static images.

If you're finding that your social life could be healthier, understand that although it may take some time to build it up again, it's more than possible to find people to build meaningful, lasting connections with. Start small and make it a habit to be friendly and chatty with everyone. Become curious about the people around you and get involved in community events. Reach out to family and reconnect with old friends you may have neglected. Smile more at people as you walk past them in the streets, and make a conscious effort to prioritize real-life interaction over texting.

Volunteer or offer your time to a charity. Speak with people who are completely *unlike* you—you could learn more from them than it first seems and give your brain a social workout. Though quiet time spent alone is regenerative, avoid moping at home by yourself. If nothing else, sit in a café where you're surrounded by people rather than alone in front of the TV. Commit to remembering people's birthdays and small details about their lives. If you're dating, try more conventional methods and don't rely exclusively on online dating apps that can be dehumanizing and stressful.

Go to community functions or join a gym or class and get chatting with the people beside you. There's no need to have a roaring time dashing all over the place—simply notice other people more and make it a habit to engage with them whenever you can. This is far easier to do if you remember that genuine and spontaneous interaction often benefits both of you and leaves the world feeling like a less lonely, less hostile place.

If we think of our brains as nothing more than machines, then we'll be tempted to imagine that all a brain does is process and manipulate objective data. So much of this "data," however, is in fact emotional in nature. If we envision our brains as tiny computers, we forget all the other things they're just as good at doing: making art, making friends, making jokes, making love, making excuses . . . The brain is not just a massive CPU, but the seat of all human ingenuity, the place our personality lives, a record of our history on this earth, a tool for communication, and a way to create poetry and music.

In the past, people thought that doing crossword puzzles was enough to "keep the mind busy." We saw the brain as something that produced, merely a kind of calculator that had mathematics and logic as its natural objects. However, a person who is socially isolated, physically unwell, and who has bad lifestyle habits and no sense of purpose or direction in life will not be healthy, cognitively or otherwise, no matter how endowed they are with intelligence or how many puzzles or brain-training games they can do. So, somewhat paradoxically, one of the best ways to boost brain health appears to be to focus on everything *but* the brain: your social life, relationships, good exercise, nutrition, and physical health.

The Best Medicine

The adage is that "laughter is the best medicine." Naturally, researchers have tried to test this idea empirically and have unsurprisingly found that a good sense of humor does in fact bode well for cognitive health, especially in older people. The study showed that participants who laughed at a funny video for twenty minutes performed better on memory tests than those who didn't watch one—not to mention the drop in cortisol levels.

Laughing reduces your blood pressure, drops your cortisol, boosts your mood, and gives your brain a pleasurable dopamine kick. Laughter actively helps you manage the daily stressors of life and can even improve your immune system, not to mention it can strengthen your social connections if done with others. This is one brain-care tip you can implement in your daily life easily today. Book a comedy night (even better, go with friends!) or watch silly videos on YouTube.

Consciously decide not to take life so seriously. Humor and creativity have a lot in common. The next time something unfortunate happens, can you change perspective and see the funny side of it? The ability to laugh at life—or yourself!—can make one incredibly resilient in the face of daily adversity or uncertainty. Be a little absurd, a little self-deprecating. Remind yourself that life is not supposed to be a painful slog—enjoy yourself. Whether this is ridiculous pranks on friends, cheesy sitcoms that always make you chuckle, or playing games with your kids, a little laughing and lightheartedness may indeed be the best medicine.

So far, we've looked at romantic relationships and sex, connections with family and community, and the value of taking it easy and laughing at it all once in a while. All of these things can add to our social health and well-being, making us feel like we're a part of the world, which in turn lowers stress and keeps our brains ticking over properly. But there's one more way in which we can be connected to the world and to others around us, and it's not something we're primed to think of all that often in the modern Western world: our ancestors.

Look Backward for a Better Future

It's probably true to say that many of us struggle in modern life to find sources of deeper meaning, a feeling of purposefulness, and the sense that we are part of something greater than ourselves. With so much focus on the future and all the goals and improvements we hope to find there, the past can be so easily forgotten.

A consequence of this is a kind of rootlessness, a lack of feeling as if one "comes from" anywhere. With globalization and people migrating internationally at record rates, many people have lost their anchoring in the traditions of their native lands, their families, and the history of those who came before them. And sadly, this can result in feeling empty and adrift in the world, not to mention utterly alone.

Far from being a relic of the past, being concerned with one's ancestry is as popular as ever, possibly explaining the rise of programs about celebrities unlocking their secret histories or DNA sequencing kits offering to tell you where your ancestors came from in millennia gone by.

No matter how abstract, sterilized, and machine-filled

our worlds have become, we all long to know who we are, where we came from, and where we're going. Many cultural anthropologists point to a big hole where our shared cultural traditions might have been in previous generations—a hole we may now fill with less-satisfying pop culture myth and obsession with celebrities.

The truth is that a huge part of our identity and sense of being comes from our *cultural* heritage. Perhaps more so for Western, individualistic societies than others, we labor to build our own "personal brands," create wealth, and develop our identities in the things we consume. But rarely does our engagement go beyond ourselves or our immediate social group. How could we understand who we are, though, unless we understand the people who came before us? The culture that created us? The very people whose genes we now carry with us?

With the rise of the ever more nuanced and complex field of epigenetics, we can begin to comprehend how our ancestors' experiences literally have been written into their DNA and passed on to subsequent generations. The unspeakable feeling you get from looking at an old family picture of someone who looks incredibly similar to you is a humbling experience. It tells us that people much like us came before, lived and learned and loved, and overcame and passed away, perhaps long before our grandparents were even born. Just beginning to contemplate some of these ideas can add a gravity and importance to life that goes beyond the petty day-to-day troubles that distract us.

Interestingly, 2011 research done by Fischer and colleagues found that students asked to think about their ancestors for five minutes felt more confident afterward about their ability to do well in their exams and overall felt more in control of their lives. What's more, they were able to perform better on a host of intelligence and cognitive tests and seemed more persistent and optimistic in tackling these tests. It's as though contemplating the challenges one's ancestors overcame gives one a confidence boost to do the same. This "ancestor effect" held even when the students imagined their ancestors more negatively—suggesting that it's simply the existence of the ancestors, and not the specific details of who they are, that improves performance. Control students asked to think about something else didn't perform as well.

Though it's an interesting effect, as always, caution should be used when interpreting it. The results do, however, hint that our brains simply function better when we have a strong sense of who we are, not just on a personal level but on a social and historical one. Feeling yourself a part of a bigger whole is grounding, and, as this research shows, may go a long way to instilling feelings of confidence, self-identity, and belonging. It's possible that this effect may hold for any activity that actively gets us to appreciate and internalize a sense that we are a valued part of a greater whole. Gain yourself some immediate perspective and sense of presence, where before you might have been occupied or bothered by things that distracted you from your main goals. In essence, this might be an instant focus booster.

If this is a phenomenon you'd like to experiment with yourself, why not start by doing the same exercise: Think about your ancestors for a moment and try to truly put yourself in their shoes, imagine their lives, and even, if you're feeling creative, talk directly to them. This is a practice employed almost universally by cultures, but it's admittedly more common in some than others.

Think for a moment about your life in the grand scheme of things. About all the events that occurred to bring you, just as you are right now in all your uniqueness, into being. Think about how much you have in common with your "tribe," despite how different you are. Think about your actions in the chain of events and how you might continue your family's legacy, even if you don't literally know their names or their stories. Imagine that you are just one petal on an unfolding bud on the tree of life, and imagine all the roots that go back in time, long before you were born.

Though you may get a temporary boost in cognitive ability, the benefits of this kind of contemplation go so much deeper. Rather than merely increasing your brain power, you may wind up bolstering your sense of self and feeling more grounded and solid in life not as a free-floating individual but a *related* being, someone with a past, a family, a group, and a shared story—even if parts of it are forgotten. It's like a social life but projected into the distant past.

Try to find subtle ways to respect and acknowledge where you've come from. Chat to the elders in your social network and show an interest in what happened before you arrived on this earth. If you can and would find it interesting, dig deeper and consider looking into your heritage more directly and fill in any gaps in the family tree. Ask older people to tell you about the past—this ordinarily fills people with dread, but this time, really *listen*. Really let it sink in that just as those people are only stories now, so, too, will you be a story one day. Paradoxically, the feeling of humbleness that comes with this realization can be incredibly freeing and encouraging.

Takeaways:

- Our identities do not come in a vacuum; we identify ourselves largely by our background, culture, and upbringing. These are all aspects of our social nature as humans: Humans are social animals, and this means that other people are an essential part of our healthy functioning and happiness. This is no different for our brains.

- Sex has been shown to improve cognitive functioning as well as overall life satisfaction and happiness (no surprise on this one). But it's a blurry assertion that the pure mechanical act of sex itself improves brain health—it is likely instead tied to the emotional, social bonding, and supportive aspects that often go hand in hand with sex. In any case, deny yourself of this natural and primal human urge to your detriment.

- On a grander scale, socialization and interaction have been shown to improve mental faculties and also battle cognitive decline in elderly people. How much is enough? That is a personal matter, but there are ways to seek out social interaction in daily life if you look for it. You might even say that without sufficient social interaction, you are depriving the brain of a need just like you would be if you had poor sleep hygiene.

- Annoyingly, just like all those inspirational posters will preach, laughter really *is* one of the best medicines.

- A surprising entry here is the power of thinking about your ancestors. It's been shown that simply pausing a moment to think about those who came before you can improve cognitive performance. Why is that? It's a social activity but not quite an interaction, yet this type of thinking has a sort of gravity that humbles you and brings perspective. More importantly, it makes you focus and concentrate on the task at hand by virtue of minimizing the importance of things that are not actually important (not an easy task in itself).

5

MENTAL SABBATICAL

A person can learn a lot about himself, the world, and his place in it by stopping for a moment to contemplate the nature of . . . well, nature. Observe the natural world for just a moment, and it's clear that things flow and move rhythmically, in cycles and undulations, coming and going, never quite the same from day to day.

Crucially, for every upswing, there's a corresponding downswing. Spring follows winter, animals sleep and then wake, things grow up out of the soil and then die back down into it again. In other words, even nature itself rests, relaxes, and takes time in every cycle to do "nothing."

We've already covered some of the reasons it's so important to consciously build sleep, recuperation, and stillness into our daily routines. It's better for your brain! Going deeper, though, the virtue of rest is often measured in terms of how productive it makes you: Take "power naps" so you can be extra efficient when you wake up. Sleep eight hours so you can go even harder at the gym the next day. Go on a retreat somewhere in the mountains so you're ultra-energized to give your best at your boring office job when you get back.

But even though it's true that rest allows for greater action, it's also something to be enjoyed for *its own sake*, not because of what we can get out of it. Sometimes, it's enough to unplug, to let go of goal-driven activity, to just "be" as we are and let the world come to us for a moment. This is the essence of deep relaxation—letting the mind and body go without grasping on to any ideas of how that should look, and embracing stillness, softness, and quietness.

Practicing calm and relaxation can be as hard as developing your focus or determination—or even harder for those Type-A personalities. In the same way that music has to be composed of both notes and the essential pauses and quiet between them, a life well lived is one of both activity and passivity in balance—otherwise, it becomes the lived equivalent of a whole lot of chaotic noise! Coincidentally, this *nothingness* has a host of benefits and boons for the brain that wishes to be boosted.

To start with, calm is the opposite of stress, which is one of the biggest detriments to the brain's health. If you want a clear and concrete illustration of this phenomenon, you don't have to look any further than any combat veteran or trauma victim suffering from post-traumatic stress disorder (PTSD) and how their lives are negatively affected. They literally lack the ability to function in daily life because they are so tense, and they are likely to snap at any given moment in response to their anxiety and fear.

A plethora of research has found that stress impacts the brain's health and mental capacity in hugely negative ways. This is in large part due to the body's physiological response to stress. But first, it will be helpful to define the difference between the two main types of stress: chronic and acute stress.

Chronic stress is when you are under ongoing stress for a relatively long period of time—something as small as being under a constant heavy load at work or dealing with a relationship that is frequently combative. These are small sources of stress that seem insignificant until you look at the cumulative effects and realize you are always on edge, testy, and tense with knots in your shoulders. When we are experiencing chronic stress (the amount of which is highly variable and relative to the person's tolerance), our body is in a state of physiological arousal. This is known as the fight-or-flight response, and it's our body's main defense mechanism when it senses a stressor.

This state was useful millennia ago when the terms "fight" and "flight" were taken literally—if the body sensed a stressor or a reason to fear, it would put itself on the highest levels of alertness and be prepared for a fight to the death, if necessary, or running away as quickly as possible. In either case, the body's hormones, heart rate, and blood pressure are highly elevated. The main stress hormone, cortisol, is released in spades and has been implicated in causing the alertness.

So if you are under chronic stress, you are permanently in this fight-or-flight mode and have spades of cortisol flowing through your system. Your body will very rarely reach the relaxation phase, which is known as a state of homeostasis. And unfortunately, cortisol impedes your mental abilities in lieu of risk analysis and critical thinking.

In other words, chronic stress makes you alert and

physiologically aroused *all the time*. This is exhausting both physically and mentally and has the effect of shrinking your brain. Studies have shown that chronic stress has caused as big as a fourteen percent decrease in hippocampal volume (the area of your brain responsible for memory encoding and storage), which is startling.

A study (Pasquali, 2006) showed that memory in rats was negatively affected when the rats were exposed to cats, which presumably caused stress. The rats that were exposed to cats far more routinely were unable to locate certain entrances and exits.

The difficult part is you may not realize you are under chronic stress because it has become normalized for you. It's just like when your shoulders tense up—you probably don't realize it until someone points it out, and you can see the contrast between being relaxed and being tense.

The cumulative effects of being constantly on edge, paranoid, unable to focus, and feeling despair and overwhelm will catch up to you. Imagine being pumped up on adrenaline for days, weeks, or months. Not only will it impair your memory and brain processing, but it will leave you unable to function in general. Excess and consistent release of cortisol can cause a loss of neurons in the prefrontal cortex and hippocampus, as well as decreasing the neurotransmitter serotonin, which is what creates the feeling of *happiness*. This is what people with PTSD suffer, but to a much higher degree.

Acute stress, on the other hand, is not something that will slide by unnoticed.

Acute stress is the sudden jolt of adrenaline you experience when someone cuts you off in traffic and you nearly crash,

83

or when you get into a heated argument. Acute stress is momentary, temporary, and you can feel it and notice it. This is when adrenaline is coursing through your veins, leaving your palms sweaty and hands shaking. Your body is trying to give you the alertness and strength you need for anything. Intense bouts of acute stress can even cause headaches, muscle tension, upset stomachs, or vomiting.

If this state persists for a longer period of time, it just may cross the threshold into chronic stress.

But the labels are unimportant. What's important is what happens to your brain's abilities when you are under any type of stress. Remember that neural changes are made with simple repetition over time. What happens when stress becomes the primary course of action?

Brain scans of stressed individuals showed less activity in the prefrontal cortex and more in the limbic system. Prolonged stress leads to structural changes—the groove is being worn in such a way that you are creating a stressed brain unable to process in any other way.

The brain literally rewires to be more efficient in conducting information through the circuits that are most frequently activated. When stress is common, these pathways can become so strong that they become your brain's fast route to its lower, reactive control centers. Your primitive brain dominates more frequently, and you lose touch with your conscious, logical, and calm brain.

So, in dealing with stress, we can return to the importance of releasing it regularly, i.e., of relaxation. There are plenty of stereotypes about what relaxation should look like, but there are no rules, as this chapter will go to show. There's no need to go to a spa or force yourself to have a picture-perfect hot bath if you actually hate them. If an activity leaves you feeling relaxed and peaceful afterward, there's no reason you can't incorporate it into your daily routine.

Video Games for a Better You

Video games, for example, frequently get categorized far away from spas and hot baths when it comes to relaxation—but they have their benefits. In 2017, the Université de Genève compiled an enormous meta-analysis of fifteen years of research into the effects of action video games (first-person shooters, etc.) on the human brain and found cognitive improvements in gamers across the board. Surprised?

Despite the negative associations that come with gaming, moderate play was shown to boost cognitive abilities—which is no surprise considering that our brain is essentially built for many of the tasks found in a typical shooter, puzzle, or racing game. In fact, in the specific metrics measured (spatial awareness and attention, multi-tasking, and adapting to new plans), the gamers were found to be better by 1.5 standard deviations than non-gamers. Quite significant.

There's also plenty of evidence that gaming enhances logical, analytical, motor, literary, executive, and even social functions in both children and adults. An hour or so spent playing a game could boost your perceptive skills, your memory, and your decision-making abilities. Gaming can slow the neurodegeneration that inevitably comes with age, lowers impulsiveness, and even has positive effects on the way the eyes process information. A 2009 study by Richard Haier and colleagues even found that a simple game like Tetris had the power to literally thicken the cortex, after introducing the game for just a three-month period to participants.

It's no surprise, really—video games force you to think quickly, to solve problems, to pay attention and process and synthesize many different strands of information at the same time. Depending on the type of game, different types of reactions, critical thinking, and problem-solving skills can be literally trained and honed. Games requiring quick thinking and action force you to adapt in one way, while those focused on deciphering puzzles and piecing together clues make you practice thinking in a completely different manner. Role-playing games encourage you to plan out your actions, predict a story, and explore possibilities.

The key is truly that at the most basic level, a video game requires a *lot* of mental engagement and focus, which keeps you alert and sharp. The brain is nothing but an adaptation machine based on what it sees and experiences, and thus, games can benefit it plenty. Play with others and you add in the skills of cooperation, communication, and leadership. Video games are not really "games" at all, but mini-worlds where people can practice all those same skills that are highly adaptive out there in the "real world"!

It's worth noting, however, that this information is not exactly a license to binge on video games or get lost in addictive gaming behavior. The researchers found positive effects at around eight or so hours a week of play, at maximum, spread out evenly across the week rather than crammed into one or two all-night gaming sessions. Like so many things in life, moderation is key here. Gaming that disrupts healthy sleeping or eating patterns, or that negatively impacts relationships and socializing, will likely cancel out any potential benefits.

If you're a gamer, periodically reassess the actual role that games are playing in your life. Be honest about why and how you play. Do you use games to procrastinate, or do you feel compelled to game to escape responsibility or avoid the rest of your life? Gaming can reduce stress, but if it's your sole defense mechanism, it can start to hinder rather than help. We live in a hyper-stimulated and addictive world filled with distractions. Is your play helping you unwind at night or making you a wired-up, antisocial insomniac? Are you able to take breaks and relax in other ways that don't require a screen?

Set a limit to how much you play and monitor yourself regularly to make sure you're using gaming as a tool for development and relaxation, rather than a drug to numb yourself or escape. Ask how you feel before and after a game. Check in with your body and your mental state, and act responsibly according to how you feel. Consider changing up the kinds of games you play as well, or recruit friends and family to play with to make it a social activity. Take breaks, don't slouch, and try to avoid pairing gaming with other unhealthy or addictive habits like snacking on junk food or drinking.

As we've already seen in the section on dopamine, gaming is one potential behavior that has the potential to turn addictive and compulsive. Not all games are created equal. Be honest about your gaming habits and answer the following questions:

- Do you find yourself playing for a lot longer than you planned to, almost as though you couldn't quit?
- Do you find that you feel angry, miserable, anxious, or "wired" after gaming in a way that takes a while to wear off?
- Do the people around you comment or even complain about your gaming behavior?
- Do you shirk duties and responsibilities in order to game, or find that you can't help but play when you should be doing something else?
- Do you find that you game almost automatically, and sometimes without even a sense of enjoyment?

If you answered yes to the above questions, chances are that gaming is not a harmless relaxation exercise. Try to dopamine detox described in an earlier chapter and see if you can recalibrate your habits around gaming. Try another game, take a long break, or limit your daily game play time.

All in all, relaxation doesn't have to be a boring chore that you add to the to-do list and begrudgingly complete because you think a healthy person ought to—in fact, this is precisely not the point! If video games honestly help you relax, play away, knowing you're using that time to chill out and train your brain at the same time.

Meditation Relaxation

If gaming isn't your style, however, there's nothing wrong with the more classically relaxing activities like meditation. Even today, meditation practice is still viewed as something rather nice you can do if you enjoy it, or if you're drawn to the vague promises of a bit more calm and composure. But it's important to realize that meditation is not strictly a *mental* activity. In fact, the more you meditate, the more you may understand it's a practice that brings together every aspect of your being—physical, emotional, spiritual, and intellectual.

Meditating can physically change the structure of your brain—a powerful reminder that when it comes down to it, we *are* our bodies, and that the body impacts the mind just as much as the mind impacts the body. Meditation can strengthen this holistic connection, and it's likely this sense of wholeness and coherence that leads to practitioners feeling more centered, less stressed, and clearer mentally.

The concept is profound: Our thoughts, or rather, our consciousness, can directly impact our physical body, including our brain. We've considered how nurturing the body supports our brain health (i.e., with exercise, sleep, and correct nutrition), but the relationship is reciprocal: A calm mind can in turn soothe the body. Thoughts of relaxation can literally translate into more relaxed biochemical states in our bodies, as well as lasting changes to the physical shapes our brains take.

As meditation and mindfulness become more mainstream, it seems like everyone meditates now, or thinks they should at least try. We won't consider the enormous spiritual or psychological benefits of meditation here in detail—by now it's well documented that people meditate because they find enormous life enrichment from tapping into the present moment, re-centering their breath, and taking a moment to still the chatter of the mind.

But meditation also has profound physical effects and, if done regularly, can be like a crash course in training your brain to perform at its best. Meditation supports all those parts of the brain that are directly linked to emotional well-being while moderating all the known effects from anxiety and stress we encounter daily.

Neuroscientist Sara Lazar (yes, again) explains in her 2011 research that meditation increases the volume, plasticity, and health of four main areas of the brain—and even shrinks one area associated with unhealthy behavior. The left hippocampus is associated with learning and memory, as well as self-awareness and empathy for others. Increasing gray matter in this area—as meditation does—will help us not only learn better but be kinder and more compassionate to others in the process.

The posterior cingulate is another area that, when larger and thicker, seems to be associated with more mental control (i.e., being able to stop a "wandering mind") and a more stable, balanced sense of self. By regularly asking the mind to focus, to return to the moment, and to not get carried away with every passing whim or thought, we get to train this area of the brain. The result is that we are able to face the rest of life more magnanimously, encountering new experiences calmly and without leaping in to identify with every passing emotion or sensation.

It may be that in the future, scientists will understand more clearly these separate functions of the mind as much as they currently comprehend the individual functions of different muscles or organs in the body. But for now, simply becoming aware of what your mind is doing and acting to be conscious of that is an excellent exercise for your consciousness, resulting in more overall mastery of your intellect and emotions—your entire lived experience.

The pons is another crucial area, and it's involved in a number of important functions, from sleep to interpreting facial expressions to motor output to coordinating data from the senses. Pons means "bridge" in Latin, and it can be thought of as having a primarily connecting and synthesizing role. As you've probably guessed, meditation strengthens the pons, helping it do its thing all the better.

The temporo-parietal junction (or TPJ), an area linked with empathy, perspective, responsibility, and just action, is likewise enhanced by meditation. Consider the ramifications. It's incredible to realize that a sense of broader perspective, of consideration for others and a feeling of compassion for beings outside yourself, can all be traced to and reflected in the activity of a region in the brain. Even more incredible is the idea that with dedicated practice and care, this area can be enhanced via meditation.

Finally, the amygdala is also physically altered by meditation—but it shrinks. The amygdala is responsible for stress, anxiety, and all those fight-or-flight responses that characterize what some Buddhists would call the ever-busy "monkey mind." As you've already guessed, meditation helps with emotional regulation and reduces stress. It's as though it allows us to consciously calm the reactive and irrational parts of our mind and strengthen our ability to look beyond ourselves, to observe without judgment, to have compassion for others, and to unhook ourselves from endless identification with fleeting stimuli, both internal and external.

It's amazing to observe that these seemingly abstract benefits of meditation are actually anchored in the physical brain and can be seen to change the body itself. With further practice, meditation will not only strengthen your body and mind, but strengthen the *relationship* they have with one another so that you can start to see them as a single unified whole under one greater, coordinating consciousness. It's true that regular meditation will probably boost your cognitive power, memory, and ability to learn and grow. But its powers go far, far beyond that, toning up not just the mental and cognitive aspects of your being, but bringing you into closer contact with a larger overarching awareness.

In the end, a calm mind is an energetic mind. We turn to the practice of mindfulness to relax the brain so that your natural state of mind is rational, nonreactive, and in energy conservation mode.

Mindfulness is the practice of purposefully focusing all your attention on the current moment and being completely aware of yourself, your emotions, and your thoughts. It can keep your mind from overthinking and running amok, which is the precursor to drained mental energy. The person who is aware of their thoughts as they are happening is far more likely to keep it together and calm versus the person who is unaware of what is taking place in the present moment.

Practicing mindfulness will feel distressing at first because people who are stressed or overwhelmed constantly feel they have too much on their plate to ever stop their minds from churning. This makes everything worse; when you're continuously moving twenty-four-seven, this gives your brain and body very little time to recharge.

Let go of the past, the future. One doesn't exist anymore, and the other may never come to be. Spending your time thinking about them is the definition of useless. And—you guessed it—a massive waste of energy because there's nothing to be done about them. Even attempt to drop what your thoughts and feelings are bound by in the present moment. Anything you can potentially be distracted by, just let it go and trust that it will be right where you left it in thirty minutes. As a last resort, make a list of these thoughts before you attempt to achieve mindfulness, and rest assured that the world will not end in the meantime.

Your focus should be only on what is happening now in your physical surroundings. Let go of what might happen later, what happened earlier, and all thoughts of the present. The only thing that matters is your breathing, your physical sensations, and the noises, sounds, smells, and sights around you.

Although it is most common to sit during meditation, you may choose to kneel or stand. Just make sure that whatever option you pick is comfortable for you to remain for thirty minutes. You can't empty your mind if your body is suffering. Ease yourself from any tension you might feel by relaxing your body as a whole and focusing your mind on the task at hand—*nothingness*.

Make sure your body is upright so that the air you breathe is easily accessible to your lungs. Inhale through your nose.

Ensure that your breaths are deep and slow. In doing so, you will allow the air you take in to go directly to your stomach, breathing the correct way for the purposes of your meditation practice.

Your mind may begin to wander from your breath, but don't chastise yourself—this is only natural. When wandering takes place, forgive, forget, move forward, and focus on your breathing. This will help you regain focus rather than wrestle with your wayward thoughts. You'll notice how easy it is for your anxieties to hijack your peace of mind and constantly jump into the mental space you've created. Instead of engaging with them and unfolding these thoughts, observe them and just let them go, then return to your breathing. We're not necessarily trying to quiet our minds, but rather center all our chatter onto one thing.

For some of us with noisier minds, you might find it more helpful to focus on a physical sensation. For instance, some will balance a cup of water on their heads (or simply hold it) because this is an act that requires the utmost concentration. Coincidentally, this is why many feel that running and other repetitive motions can create a meditative state. You can also move through your body limb by limb and feel the sensations present in each part.

Let go. Enjoy the break from the outside pressures you face daily. Reboot your brain and eliminate all the clutter that was preventing you from thinking clearly or being self-aware. Think about how the air feels on your lips, in your nose, and moving down your throat. Focus on the sound of inhalation and exhalation.

If this sounds too simplistic to be effective, you're in for a surprise. At the core, this process is where mindfulness comes from. Your brain gains a rare reprieve from its efforts as the proverbial mouse on a wheel. Your body is able to reset ever so slightly to a state of homeostasis and relaxation. You receive perspective on your anxieties and understand that you are not forced to be overwhelmed—it was your choice all along. And this is a key element to boosting your brain and keeping yourself primed for success.

Passively Consuming Your Favorite Media

And now, to move on to something you may not have considered a "proper" relaxation technique: watching TV. Along with video games, sitting in front of the TV is frequently considered mind-numbing at worst and a waste of time at best. But Professor Kevin Warwick at Reading University, a cyberneticist and speaker on the way humans interface with technology, claims that watching TV is not the brain-dead activity we sometimes accuse it of being, but even better for us than listening to classical music or doing a crossword. He presented his findings in the 2004 Chartered Institute of Personnel and Development, along with other ideas.

Students who were asked to perform cognitive tests before and after a TV-watching session showed a statistically significant increase in IQ of five points—and curiously, this effect was more pronounced in women. The *kind* of TV program also played a role, but it's likely that more research is needed to understand exactly why this is and what it means. Though a five-point IQ increase might not seem like much, a small and temporary intellectual boost like this might be just the thing before an important exam or event that requires your best performance. At the very least, it will leave you feeling far less stressed than cramming with a book until the last minute!

Speaking of books, Warwick actually found that curling up with something to read for a half hour *decreased* intellectual capacity—something that would certainly give your old teachers and parents pause. But could this possibly be true? Could watching TV really be better for you than reading?

Well, the answer is probably quite complex. We do have plenty of evidence to suggest that as far as brain-healthy habits go, reading is as good as it gets. It's difficult to overstate the many benefits of reading—a person who reads exercises their mind and imagination, expands their horizons, and develops their ability to focus carefully for long periods.

Beyond the actual mechanics of reading words on a page, reading books opens doors to profound ideas and new worlds—anything you like, really. Perhaps we all appreciate the value of reading because it's so much alike to thinking; when we read, we talk to ourselves mentally, we imagine, create, form ideas and opinions, even converse in a way with the author or the characters they create. We turn concepts over, play with images and words, and overall share in the great buffet of different perspectives that are out there in the world. The right kind of TV certainly contains these kinds of elements, so it turns out that we can't just write things off completely.

Perhaps what makes reading seem so wonderful is that is

positions your brain as an active participant rather than a mere observer who cannot engage with the content. When you read, your brain is hard at work interpreting symbols, synthesizing concepts, ticking along to weave the most complex and abstract mental images from nothing more than marks on a page—remarkable, when you think about it. While you sit quietly, your brain is whizzing along like an orchestra conductor, rapidly stitching together a dynamic inner experience that will be unlike anyone else's.

Reading is a part of human heritage—manipulating language and symbols this way is so characteristically human that it's built into the very structure of our brains. In fact, reading about an event and actually experiencing it both activate the same regions in the brain—in other words, reading is not just an intellectual activity.

Despite Warwick's observations, many more scientists have found that regular reading has profound benefits for our brains. David Comer Kidd and Emanuele Castano designed research in 2013 that seems to show that reading literary fiction drastically improves people's "theory of mind." This is basically the ability of the human mind to comprehend that other people have realities—beliefs, experiences, desires—different from one's own that motivate them. Naturally, reading narrative fiction encourages the consideration of other perspectives and inner worlds, enhancing empathy and imagination in the process.

This boost in emotional intelligence is also why socializing is so good for us—it forces us out of our own narrow cognitive limits and allows us to "try on" different mental modes, gaining a new understanding and perspective on our own. The benefits for relationships and creativity are obvious. A 2011 Stanford study by Raymond Mar showed overlap in the regions involved in both storytelling and social interactions. This "fluid intelligence" is about improving your emotional capacity to comprehend others. In reading, we learn how to listen to others, to interpret, to synthesize random units and events into a coherent and deeply meaningful narrative.

Reading a good book is like having a good conversation—it can help us understand who we are, learn more about the world, enrich our thinking and feeling, and perhaps best of all, offer up a stylized, novel world to our imaginations that's valuable simply because it engrosses us. Reading can help us do all the other things we've identified as beneficial—be sociable, relax, even connect with ancestors.

Most activities in our modern routines are scattered, forcing us to split our attention and multitask. But reading is about sustained, focused concentration. It's quietly meditative, this choice to actively zone out the rest of the world, and makes you an active participant rather than someone constantly and passively reacting to the next phone ping, or browsing online for the next distraction. Give your attention span a workout by pushing yourself to focus on reading for longer and longer periods. In a world of instant gratification and an internet designed to bombard you with a never-ending conveyer belt of stimuli, choose to actively go in *depth* with reading, slowing down and taking the time to properly engage with each new word one at a time.

Much like watching TV, the benefits of reading likely depend on the *kind* of material we read. There is nothing innately beneficial about physically moving your eyes over a printed page or intellectually comprehending the meaning it holds. In fact, reading can be tiring and cause eye strain! Rather, the benefits are all about the deeper significance, the point of the story, the new information gleaned, and how that relates to our own lives.

If you'd like to reap the benefits of reading, start by finding material you're genuinely interested in. There's no point forcing yourself to read a "classic" that you actually find boring. You don't even have to read fiction. Pick material that you find yourself wanting to read, then allot some time every single day to be quiet and simply read. Start with fifteen minutes or so and push yourself to read more and more as your attention span improves. Eventually, you may find yourself knocking out an hour of reading without even noticing.

You're more likely to get reading done if you build it into your everyday routines. Read every day on the train to work. Put a book next to your bed so you can read for twenty minutes before bed every evening. Dedicate a quiet room in your house as the "reading corner" and combine it with other self-care habits like a nice cup of herbal tea, meditation, or just contemplating the sound of the wind outside. Try a Kindle or eReader, and experiment with new authors, new ideas, new formats. Avid readers don't read out of a sense of responsibility or because they're hoping to improve their brain power. Rather, they're driven by curiosity and enjoyment, and their boost in intelligence is merely a side effect to help them keep up.

Considering all these ways to relax—some less conventional

than others—might have you thinking that your daily routine is a little more useful than you previously gave it credit for. While many of us tend to dismiss time spent goofing off or watching nonsense on TV, why not reframe this time as beneficial for your brain? Time off from the overly analytical, mechanical, and calculating mode of living allows other aspects to emerge—creative thinking, relaxation, intuition, and appreciation and joy.

Have a Lay

In fact, if you'd like to encourage the more creative aspects of your cognition, just sit back and relax. Literally. Dr. Darren Lipnicki, of the school of psychology in the Faculty of Science at ANU, has shown in a preliminary study that certain cognitive tasks are performed more easily when people are lying down, or "supine."

Participants experienced the answers to an anagram unscrambling puzzle as though "out of the blue" when lying down, suggesting that their brains passively and unconsciously solved the problem for them, in a kind of *eureka* moment. Perhaps Freud was on to something when he suggested that patients lie flat on a sofa as they receive psychotherapy. There are countless scientists who credit more nontraditional activities like these in helping them reach breakthroughs or novel insights.

Perhaps you yourself have experienced it: You work diligently for ages on solving a problem only to find that the answer comes to you much later, entirely unbidden and when you are focusing on something else. Salvador Dali is said to have exploited this creative process by allowing himself to fall asleep upright in a chair. He would hold a spoon loosely in his hand and place a plate underneath it. When he drifted off to sleep, his grip loosened, the spoon came crashing down onto the plate, and he instantly awoke to quickly note down the weird and wonderful images that had flooded his mind on that cusp between waking and sleep.

If you want to tap into your brain's creativity, just sit back and relax. Lipnicki explains that this helps because noradrenaline, a neurotransmitter that normally inhibits creative problem solving, is reduced when we lie down. The result is the ability to experience those "out of the blue" flashes of insight. Crucially, this process seemed not to hold for arithmetic problems, which are unlike "insight problems" such as the anagram task. It's these insight tasks that are more likely to be solved in one sudden moment of awareness when lying down, or even in sleep or other deeply relaxed states of mind.

Even though this study was only a preliminary one, it probably wouldn't hurt to remember the role of posture when studying, reading, or problem-solving. Anecdotally, many people find they can shift creative blocks or make cognitive breakthroughs simply by taking a deep breath, getting up and moving around, lying down, or changing their position in the room. It would seem that we can get a fresh perspective on a challenging problem by *literally* changing the way we look at it, or how our body is positioned in relation to it. So the next time you're at your desk, trying to work your head around something new or challenging, mix it up a little: Go lie down for a few minutes and see if the problem looks a little different all of a sudden.

Takeaways:

- Sometimes a mental sabbatical is just what you need. Actually, this should be an essential part of your daily, weekly, and monthly routine. We all need to disconnect and recharge; our brains are incapable of functioning at a high level without that rest. Consider this chapter in combination with the chapter on neurofitness, and once again, the holistic mind-body connection cannot be ignored and must be cultivated.

- When it comes to relaxing, there are a few methods that run counter to what you might assume is most helpful. Some people just want to turn into a vegetable on the couch, and that works to a certain degree. But video games, television, and reading are all excellent ways of combining rest, relaxation, and beneficial mental engagement. They all emphasize different modes of thought—video games force you to adapt to quicker reaction speeds and problem-solving; reading and television allow you to inhabit the minds of others. The media itself is not important, actually; it's just that it is pleasurable mental engagement that leaves you feeling better about yourself after the fact.

- Practicing meditation and mindfulness is the most predictable tip for relaxation. Stop ruminating on the past or the future. Try to not even focus on the present. Attempt to clear your mind and think only about one thing, such as your breathing. It sounds like the easiest thing in the world, and yet, you'll struggle to do it. But pursuing this seemingly tiny goal will result in massive neurological changes that will improve your resistance to stress and anxiety and wire your system for more resilience.

6

PROTECT YOUR BRAIN FROM STRESS

Your Brain on Stress

Trying to maintain cognitive and mental health is a futile effort if you are constantly stressed. All the healthy habits and brain training in the world cannot undo the effect of chronic stress on the body and mind. Neuroscience is finding increasing evidence for just how bad stress is for the brain.

The word "stress" covers many different experiences, from anxieties around work, family, and personal life, to worries about money or relationships. What they all have in common, however, is that they are *perceived to be a threat* in some way, and because of this perception, the body goes into automatic fight-or-flight mode.

This emergency response emerged in our earliest ancestors as a protective mechanism—but it was always meant to kick in during extreme, unusual, and *short-lived* situations. When the fight-or-flight mechanism is overstimulated for a period longer than it was ever designed for (i.e., when we experience chronic stress), then problems develop, such a depression, anxiety, burnout, or physical symptoms like headaches or insomnia.

Before we dive in and explore ways to protect your brain from stress (which is an eternal and natural part of everyday life, but one that can nevertheless be managed and moderated), let's take a closer look at some of the signs that stress may be taking its toll on you and your brain.

Stress Increases Mental Illness

In a paper published in *Molecular Psychiatry* (Chetty et al., 2014), researchers discovered that chronic stress can lead to a greater risk of developing mood disorders later in life, such as depression or anxiety. A 2015 study by Yang et al. went on to say that stress may actually play a big role in how these psychiatric disorders develop in the first place. How?

One theory is that ongoing stress results in fewer neurons being produced in the brain, while at the same time, more myelin-producing cells are created. The excess myelin can actually interfere with the function of the brain and the way the nerve cells communicate with one another.

Stress Damages Brain Structure

It's so easy to think of stress as a purely psychological phenomenon, but it actually has a primarily physiological basis. Never-ending stress can literally change the structure of your brain! As we've already seen, the brain contains both white matter and gray matter. The white matter is made of the myelin-coated neural axons, which are like telephone wires connecting up various parts of the brain. The white color is due to the myelin, which is essentially a form of fat. The gray matter is the neurons themselves plus the cells that support them. This part of the brain is responsible for all higher order thinking and decision-making.

In a paper titled, "White Matter Abnormalities in Post-traumatic Stress Disorder Following a Specific Traumatic Event" (Li et al., 2016), researchers discovered that people experiencing symptoms of PTSD (post-traumatic stress disorder) tend to have an imbalanced ratio of white to gray matter. This strongly suggests that extreme or chronic stress could literally make its mark on your brain's structure—which would alter how you were able to face subsequent challenges, too.

It's not just the extreme, single stressful events that can harm our brains, however. A background of low-grade but constant stress may prove more damaging in the long run—in the same way that drops of water can over time bore holes through rocks that even strong floods can't wash away.

Psychologist Daniela Kaufer adds that not all stress is created equal—"good stress" can help the brain adapt in the face of challenge, whereas chronic, ongoing stress can undermine your resilience over time and make you more predisposed to developing mental illness. With stress, "you're creating a brain that's either resilient or very vulnerable to mental disease, based on the patterning of white matter you get early in life," explained Kaufer in a news release.

Stress Destroys Brain Cells

A study conducted at the Rosalind Franklin University of Medicine and Science found that a single stress event could literally kill new nerve cells in the hippocampus (Thomas et al., 2007). In the experiment, rats exposed to stressful aggression from other rats showed cortisol levels six times higher than rats who did not have this experience. Interestingly, these rats did tend to grow the same number of new neurons; however, fewer of the new neurons were still alive one week later when compared to non-stressed rats.

They concluded that stress doesn't impact neurogenesis (the birth of new neurons) but that it certainly impaired their survival. The researchers are now investigating whether antidepressants might help keep alive the new neurons in the brains of chronically stressed people . . . but for now, this is just a theory.

Stress Causes Brain Shrinkage

...at least in those areas responsible for emotional regulation, memory, and overall metabolism. Yikes!

A Yale University study quizzed one hundred healthy study participants about the stress they'd endured in life, then examined their brains. They found that exposure to stress was correlated with less overall gray matter in the pre-frontal cortex—i.e., smaller brains overall (Ansell et al., 2012). Even if everyday stresses appear not to be causing any trouble at the moment, they may still make the brain more vulnerable in the future so that when a very extreme stress event *is* encountered, more brain damage and shrinkage result than if the brain had been more resilient.

Emily Ansel, the project lead, explained that "the accumulation of stressful life events may make it more challenging for these individuals to deal with future stress, particularly if the next demanding event requires effortful control, emotion regulation, or integrated social processing to overcome it."

Stress Impairs Memory

Finally, you probably won't be surprised to learn that all this adds up to a brain that has trouble remembering things. You've probably experienced it yourself in the moment: Feeling stressed out and flustered makes it so much more difficult to remember tiny dates and details . . . or remember where you put your keys just a minute ago.

A study conducted in rats concluded that high levels of cortisol, the stress hormone, were correlated with short-term memory loss, especially in older rats (Anderson et al., 2014). Another study found that chronic stress can impact spatial memory—which is both the ability to recall the location of objects as well as orient in space; that is—it's not your keys you lose, but yourself! (Conrad, 2010).

Though none of the above findings are in the least surprising, it is sobering to grasp that our lifestyle, our environments, and to some extent, our perceptions and attitudes can create lasting changes to our brain anatomy. How do we avoid the literal brain damage caused by too much stress? That's easy: reduce stress!

Control Your Breath and Arousal

Your breath and your mood are intimately connected. Have you noticed how when you're stressed or angry, you also seem to be breathless? And when you're relaxed and calm (even sleeping), your breath rate is slow and deep?

We can use knowledge of the connection between breath and arousal to help us calm down and regulate our stress levels, protecting our brain.

Deep breathing (also called abdominal breathing, diaphragmatic breathing, or "belly breathing") deliberately links up your conscious awareness with your breath. And your breath is connected to your body. That means with deep breathing, we are giving ourselves the opportunity to use our *mind* to consciously control and regulate our *body* responses—in particular, the response of stress.

Deep breathing practice has many benefits:

- Slower heart rate and lowered blood pressure
- More relaxation and feelings of wellbeing
- Better sleep quality
- Improved moods, i.e., lower levels of depression and anxiety
- Improved digestion
- Better oxygenation of the entire body, which in turn improves the immune system, endurance, wounds healing, and so much more

Let's explore four powerful and evidence-backed deep breathing techniques that can help us reduce the effects of stress on the brain.

Technique 1: Breath Focus

When you focus on your breath with quiet, mindful attention, you halt any inner dialogue that may be sustaining stress and worry. Stress and anxiety are often based in thoughts about the past or the future, but by focusing on the breath, we bring ourselves square in the present moment, where there is usually very little to be truly anxious about.

Here's how to practice a breath focus exercise any time you're feeling a little overwhelmed with stress or anxiety:

1. Pick a "mantra," which can simply be a single word like "peace" or "I am calm."
2. Find a comfortable position somewhere, sitting or lying, where you won't be interrupted.
3. You might like to stretch a little to warm up and get comfortable, although this is not necessary.
4. Place one hand on your chest and one on your lower belly.
5. Now inhale slowly through your nose in such a way that you can feel the hand on your belly rise while the hand on your chest stays where it is. Take a few seconds to do this inhale, hold a moment, and then exhale for two seconds through the mouth.
6. As you exhale, mentally say your mantra.

7. Repeat at least ten times, but preferably more, feeling your breath deepen and slow each time. You can experiment with making inhales and exhales longer or lengthening the pause between. Just keep things as slow and even as possible.

8. Focus intently on your five senses as you go, and imagine the air flowing into and out of your body and into each and every corner of every cell of every organ.

This is an excellent way to stop racing thoughts and halt an anxiety spiral or even panic attack. If stressful thoughts pop into your mind, gently set them aside and place all your attention on the act of inhaling and exhaling. Focus on the sound of your breath, the slight feeling of warmth around your nostrils, the texture of your jumper under your resting hand, and so on.

Technique 2: Lion's Breath

This exercise comes from a pranayama pose in yoga and is intended to be stimulating and energizing. Flooding the body with oxygen in this way and expanding the lungs is so invigorating that the technique is often used by performers before going on stage.

Interestingly, this exercise is also said to boost self-esteem and remove stubborn feelings of shame and guilt. If your stress has a lethargic, doom-and-gloom feeling to it, you may find lion's breath very helpful! Here's how to do it:

1. Find a comfortable position and stretch a little to warm up.
2. Lean forward and place your hands on your knees.
3. Inhale deeply through the nose, filling both your belly and your lungs with plenty of fresh, clean air.
4. Now—here's the fun part—open your mouth as wide as possible, your chin stretched far toward the floor and your tongue stuck out as far as it will go, and exhale forcibly, making a deep growling HA! noise (just like a lion). Go all out and make this sound as forceful as possible.
5. For the next sixty seconds or so, return to normal breathing, then repeat the lion's breath.
6. Try around five to ten full lion's breath repetitions, letting it all go and putting as much energy into your exhale as possible.

Yes, the lion's breath exercise is definitely silly-looking and probably best done alone, but it almost always peps you up, gets your mind out of stale old loops and ruts, and forces oxygenated air into your body. This is a great technique to combine with other stretching techniques and can help clear mental blocks and stubborn, repetitive behavior.

Technique 3: Humming Bee Breath

Also called *bhramari*, this technique is great for releasing negative emotions that can linger as stress and anxiety that damage your brain in the long term. Sometimes, unprocessed events or unresolved thoughts and negative beliefs can linger on in the body and in the brain, causing the chronic release of stress hormones. But the humming and vocal vibration of this technique can soothe these negative emotions, stimulate the vagus nerve (which will promote emotional regulation), and calm the central nervous system:

1. Find a comfortable seated or lying down position.
2. Close your eyes and spend a few moments imagining calm and relaxation washing over you. Try a few visualizations if you like, such as picturing a golden light showering peaceful rays over you, or imagining that the day's stress and worries are literally floating out of and away from your body.
3. Place the index and middle finger of each hand on the fleshy nub of cartilage that partially covers the opening of your ear canal.
4. Inhale deeply and fully and, on exhaling through the nose, hum out loud. Take the time to convert all the air of your exhale into a humming vibration.
5. Pause at the end of the exhale and repeat up to five more times.
6. Spend a few moments beathing normally and focusing on your body. Open your eyes.

Humming bee breath might not seem like much until you try it; the vibrations you created by humming have a shooting and regulating effect on the vagus nerve, which is the major nerve connecting your brain to the rest of your body. Once you have some practice, try mixing things up by combining your exhale with a loud, spoken chant or mantra. Even the classic "om" can center the mind and create soothing vibrations that ground and calm you.

Technique 4: Box Breathing

Breath control is arousal control, i.e., the trained ability to control the physiological state of arousal through control of the breath. According to Mark Divine in *Unbeatable Mind*, masterful respiratory control is the primary way to achieve mental toughness and resilience. He discovered that the same breathing technique used by elite athletes and highly trained Navy SEALs would allow him to maintain self-control during even extremely stressful situations.

When you're stressed or anxious, you go into fight-or-flight mode, your adrenaline and cortisol levels spike, your heart rate leaps, and your muscles tighten up to prepare to act. These are all adaptations that genuinely help us survive . . . but they can also make us bad thinkers. But by using Divine's "box breathing," you can purposefully take charge of the situation and control your nervous system from the outside in:

1. Inhale through your nose and deep into your belly for five seconds (you can count "one Mississippi" to measure one second).
2. Hold your breath for five seconds.
3. Exhale through the mouth, making the breath last five seconds.
4. When all the air is expelled, hold your breath for five seconds before starting again.

It's easy enough to be grounded and meditative when everything is just fine; box breathing, however, is a great technique to use during a stressful or challenging time. Perhaps there is an emergency or you need to think fast. Maybe you're upset and scared but need to put that aside so you can act wisely. Box breathing will help put you in the best possible frame of mind to make the right decisions.

Control Your Emotions and Thoughts

While your breath, your state of physiological arousal, and your stress levels are all connected, we cannot ignore the role that emotions and thoughts play, not only in creating stress out of thin air, but in influencing the way we interpret, deal with, and recover from the inevitable challenges of life. We will finish this chapter by looking at three key ways that you can master and control your own cognitive and emotional reality, thereby getting a handle on stress.

Affect Labeling

Affect labeling is simply the ability to put words to the feelings you're experiencing. While the temptation can be to ignore or escape unpleasant emotions (or even the opposite, indulge in them!), the research shows that *naming* how we feel is the best approach. When we do this, we simply notice what is happening, without clinging or resisting.

Psychologist and author of *Social: Why Our Brains Are Wired to Connect*, Matthew Lieberman found that when study participants were asked to label their emotions, there was less overall recorded brain activity in their amygdalas. The team hypothesized that labeling created psychological distance that allowed for better emotional regulation since emotions then became objects that we could step back from and look at.

Putting feelings into words boosts emotional self-regulation but also influences how you experience that emotion and can even moderate autonomic processes in the body such as heart rate, breathing, and activity in the brain. When we label an emotion, we suddenly create a little moment of autonomous awareness and self-reflection—at the very least, we may temporarily distract ourselves from the intensity of the emotion, meaning we don't prolong it unnecessarily.

Affect Labeling Changes Your Experience

One study (Burklund et al., 2014) asked participants to look at some emotionally charged images such as a snake or a disturbing hospital scene. One group was asked to simply look at these images, while a second group was asked to view the images but simultaneously label the emotions they felt and what they were experiencing.

The participants who did affect labeling were recorded as experiencing less negative arousal and what the researchers called "negative valence" compared to those who did not label their emotions. Simply putting a word on what you are feeling can actually have physiological effects, with affect labeling apparently influencing cardiovascular reactivity, heart rate, and skin conductance.

Affect Labeling May Be Better than Distraction, Exposure, or Reappraisal

A 2012 study by Kircanski et al. published in the journal *Psychological Science* concluded that of three different emotional "downregulation" strategies, affect labeling may be the most effective. The researchers asked participants who experienced arachnophobia (fear of spiders) to spend some time near a tarantula in a cage. One group simply endured the tarantula, while three other groups also engaged in one of three emotional regulation strategies: distraction, reappraisal, or affect labeling.

The group told to label their emotions showed greater reductions in their psycho-physiological arousal levels than the other groups. In fact, this result seemed to persist even one week later, when these participants were able to move closer to the tarantula.

Affect Labeling Can Change Your Behavior

In the above study, the participants with arachnophobia were actually able to take action inspired by their new sense of mastery and self-awareness around their emotion—they moved closer to the thing that had previously terrified them. In another study (Ramirez, Beilock, 2011), researchers found that when students took the time to write about their anxieties around an upcoming math exam, they actually performed better on the test.

Perhaps this is because once the students were able to acknowledge their fears, they were free to actually do something about them—i.e., study hard and prepare better.

Why does affect labeling have so many interesting effects? Torre and Lieberman claim it comes down to four things:

1. When you label emotions, you're **distracted**, i.e., you interfere with the experience of the emotion to talk about the emotion, which creates a gap and a distance from that emotion. The emotion is dampened, and you're better able to cope with it.

2. When you label emotions, you gain an opportunity for **self-reflection**. This introspection can create awareness and understanding, which slows activity in the amygdala and prefrontal cortex. The emotion is still there, but somehow, it's not so all-encompassing.

3. When you label your emotions, you reduce uncomfortable feelings of **uncertainty** or confusion. There's a sense of control and order that comes with nailing down what may be a very nebulous and vague feeling. Suddenly, the emotion seems smaller and more manageable.

4. Converting emotions into language involves a kind of **symbolic abstraction** that calls on the brain's higher processing functions and pulls attention away from more primal, automatic responses. You're no longer enmeshed in the experience but standing outside of it and looking in.

How can you use affect labeling for yourself? According to Torre and Lieberman in a 2018 article published in the journal *Emotion Review*, there are three main ways:

1. **Be curious and notice:** Pause and pay attention to what is going on. Literally ask yourself, "What am I feeling right now?"

2. **Write it down:** When you write, you slow down and are forced to find the right words. You see your experience down there, outside of your head and on the page.

3. **Speak up:** If you happen to be in an emotionally tense conversation, you might like to pause a moment and try to say out loud how you are feeling. Now, this needs to be done simply and not as a weapon or an accusation. "I feel so confused" is great, whereas "you're confusing me" is less so! Even if you can't quite explain what is going on with you, merely shifting to "I feel" language signals a vulnerability and willingness to connect that in itself can defuse difficult conversations.

   Of course, if you're truly overwhelmed and flooded with strong emotions, you can also choose to consciously call an end to the conversation and return to it later, when you're feeling calmer and clearer. In that case, you can contemplate or write down your feelings in your own time.

As you gain more practice at learning to label your emotions, you might become aware of the fact that it's never possible to perfectly describe an emotional state with words alone. The real human depths of our experiences are sometimes difficult to articulate, and when we use words to talk about them, something is inevitably "lost in translation."

However, just because affect labeling can vary in its accuracy, it doesn't mean that it doesn't have any value, both for personal self-regulation and for better communication with others. A few words of warning, however. When you label your emotions, try to avoid heaping on shame or blame or judgment. When you *accuse* yourself of feeling an emotion, play *gotcha!*, harshly diagnose yourself, or make a value judgment about what that emotion means, you are likely to make the experience far worse!

For example, avoid saying things like, "I'm feeling weak and pathetic," or, "I'm having stupid fears about XYZ." Instead, try a more neutral observation like, "I feel vulnerable," or, "I'm anxious." Likewise, don't get carried away with complex interpretations and loaded sentiments about what should or shouldn't be the case. So, rather than saying, "I'm feeling neurotic and irrational" (one is a loaded and vague psychiatric term, and another is a judgment—neither are really emotions), say instead, "I'm scared," or, "I'm feeling angry about this, but at the same time, I can't think of a good reason why."

By sticking to neutral labels, you gain psychological distance; if you accidentally squeeze in some blame, shame, or judgment, though, you actually reduce that distance and get even more tangled up in the emotions you're trying to manage.

One final way that affect labeling can improve your life is indirectly, i.e., through your ability to downregulate and manage *other people's* emotions. When you have enough presence of mind to correctly acknowledge and label what another person is feeling, you communicate empathy and understanding, you defuse difficult situations, and you show that you're listening. Of course, the old "no blame, shame, or judgment" rule applies even more so here. Nobody wants to be bluntly told how they're feeling, especially if it's leveled as an attack, accusation, or smug way to gain superiority.

The next time you're in a difficult conversation or even an argument, *gently suggest* how the other person might be feeling—in fact, you might want to ask and not tell. For example, "You seem really uncertain at the moment. Have I got that right?" rather than, "You're confused." Don't be afraid to come right out and ask how the other person is feeling. Sometimes, difficult conversations skirt endlessly around the elephant in the room, which is a difficult emotion. Once you acknowledge this emotion, you take the conversation to a different, more human level and have a better chance of finding a resolution.

Learn to Reframe Your Thoughts

Your brain possesses an almost supernatural ability called **neuroplasticity**. In short, this means that it can continually reorganize its synaptic connections, breaking down old ones to build new ones. This is what allows the brain to heal after injury, and it's exactly what happens whenever we learn or adapt or grow. It also means that even if our brain is currently wired along certain neural pathways, *it is always possible to change them*.

Every day, your brain is filled with countless thoughts—chances are most of these thoughts are negative, repetitive, or inaccurate. Where did these thoughts come from? Well, your current brain setup is a complex result of past learning experiences and influences that come from your environment, together with ingrained thought patterns, beliefs, and traits.

Let's say you have a negative experience in childhood that leaves you mistrustful of others. The thought *the world isn't safe* gets cemented in your brain, and every time you encounter evidence that supports it, that neural pathway gets stronger. It gets so strong, in fact, that you barely notice it's there at all. While it's true that your brain originally wired up that way in response to an external trauma, many years later, it might be your own unconscious thought patterns and processes that keep this belief going . . . as well as resist any alternative beliefs.

Human beings have actually been found to have a "negativity bias," i.e., we focus more intently on those events in our environment that are negative or could threaten us. This makes sense in evolutionary terms—it's worth paying close attention to what could potentially kill you! One result of this bias, however, is that negative events, thoughts, and beliefs tend to dominate our thinking.

But there is also evidence that this negativity is taught rather than innate. Research done in the 1980s (Campos et al., 1981) showed that when an infant was primed to interpret a neutral event as positive, they did so, whereas when they were primed to expect the event to be negative, that's exactly what they did. So, whilst human beings certainly do have a primal and innate need to survive potential threats, we also begin life by looking to our caregivers to tell us what to consider a threat in the first place.

It is not the environment that determines our thoughts or our socialization, but rather a blend of the two. Combined with neuroplasticity, this means we have the power to re-socialize ourselves and change how we interpret our environment (Walden, Ogden, 1988, *The Development of Social Referencing*).

What has this got to do with stress?

When your brain encounters a potential threat, a cascade of physiological processes begins, setting off hormonal and chemical reactions in the body to allow for a fight-or-flight response. But how your brain *interprets* this physiological arousal has more to do with your culture, your upbringing, and your personal history. The body may release cortisol and adrenaline, but it is the mind that puts these experiences into context and makes them mean something.

Hans Selye was a physician who introduced the General Adaptation Syndrome, or GAS theory, to explain how the body responds and adapts to stress. He said that first there would be alarm, followed by resistance, and then finally exhaustion. For example, the alarm phase is the racing heart and constricted muscles, the resistance phase is when the body attempts to adjust and repair itself in response to this stress. But if this resistance is prolonged, exhaustion results.

Putting it all together, we can see that certain maladaptive responses to stress can be ingrained into the brain by a combination of innate negativity bias together with socialization and the interpretation of the mind. We cannot do much about our evolutionary inheritance, but because the brain is plastic, we *can* do a lot to change our brains by changing the way we think. This is the process of reframing thoughts.

It's not the event, but your thought about the event

A core tenet of cognitive behavioral therapy (CBT) is that human beings are capable of identifying their maladaptive thoughts and consciously replacing them with healthier, more balanced, and more useful thoughts. If we can identify cognitive distortions (such as the negativity bias, which makes reality appear more negative than it strictly is), then we can literally rewire our brains for the better.

Stress can profoundly damage the brain, but some of this damage stems not from the event itself, but our interpretation of it. In his book *Feeling Good*, Dr. David Burns explains several common cognitive distortions that can create unnecessary stress for us and harm our brains:

- **All-or-nothing**, black-and-white thinking that accepts no complexity or nuance. ("Either I succeed at this today or I'll be a failure forever.")
- **Discounting the positive**, where we focus on the bad and ignore or minimize the good. ("The good grades I've gotten so far don't really count—only the test that I flunked badly matters.")
- **Jumping to conclusions**, i.e., reaching an unfounded conclusion based on little (or no) evidence. ("She said she's too busy to meet up today; she probably doesn't want to be friends at all.") This distortion often goes with **mindreading**, where we wrongly assume we understand people's thoughts, feelings, or motivations when we have zero grounds to do so.
- **Emotional reasoning** is where we come to conclusions

based not on evidence or reason at all, but purely by our emotions, usually the negative ones. ("That waiter was a little rude to me; I bet it's because they're judging what I ordered for lunch.")

- **Catastrophizing** is blowing the legitimately negative out of proportion. ("I've been dumped; I'm utterly unlovable and will never meet anyone in this life!")

Reframing these unnaturally negative (and stressful!) thoughts into something more positive and balanced takes effort and time but will eventually help you rewire your brain. Here's one way:

Step 1: Start by Being Aware

Just notice what your negative self-talk is like and become curious about whether it's distorted. Just because you have a thought doesn't mean you have to act on it, take it as true, or respond in any way! Just notice.

Example: Your partner is late and you notice the thought, "Maybe they've had a fatal car crash."

Step 2: Look at the Evidence

Without judgment, try to look at the neutral, objective facts of the situation. Imagine you were a third party observing things from afar; how would you describe it? If you genuinely don't know, acknowledge that rather than guess.

Example: You look at the facts and remember that car crashes are not super common and that your partner is only ten minutes late, which could be explained by dozens of more likely causes. You also realize that you currently have zero evidence to assume the worst outcome.

Step 3: Look at the Thought Again

Compared against the facts, is your original thought accurate?

Can you recognize any cognitive distortions?

Consider also whether it is useful, i.e., does it help you achieve what you want to achieve? Become curious about the overall outcome of believing this thought. How does it make you think, act, and feel? Do you want to continue thinking, acting, and feeling this way?

Example: You look again at the car crash idea and realize that while it's a possibility, it's exaggerated, and that catastrophizing this way stresses you out. You don't want to feel that way!

Step 4: Rewrite the Thought

With compassion and patience, gently challenge the thought and replace it with something better.

Example: You rewrite the thought in your mind there and then, telling yourself, "I don't know why my partner is ten minutes late, but chances are she's fine, and me worrying about it will not change the situation either way."

Takeaways:

- It is difficult if not impossible to maintain healthy, resilient brain health in the face of chronic stress. Ongoing low-grade stress is associated with mental illness and can literally damage the structures of the brain for the long term. Stress can kill newly formed brain cells and even lead to brain shrinkage, as well as interfere with memory.

- One way to reduce stress is by learning to control arousal via breath control. Deep belly breathing can lower central nervous system arousal and regulate stress levels, protecting our brain.

- Try simply focusing on slow, deep, and controlled breathing for a few moments, or practice the more energizing "lion's breath" yogic exercise, the soothing and balancing "humming bee" practice, or the mind-clearing Navy SEAL "box breathing" technique.

- Another important way to manage the body's stress response is to become mindful of your thoughts and emotions, and challenge and rewrite distorted thoughts patterns that are creating stress for you.

- One proven method is affect labeling, or putting words to the emotion you're feeling. This can create psychological distance, distract you, allow you a reappraisal of the situation, and even change how you act in response. Simply notice without judgment how you're feeling, write it down, or share your observation with others in conversations.

- You can also reframe certain thoughts and counteract the innate human negativity bias. The brain is neuroplastic and can be trained to interpret neutral stimuli differently. First become aware of a negative thought and then compare it against your values, your goals, and any objective evidence, opting if necessary for a healthier alternative that is less distorted.

7

TRUE BRAIN TRAINING

By now, it's more than clear that maintaining cognitive and mental health has a lot more to it than we previously assumed. In essence, everything discussed here is an attempt to master and optimize the brain's neuroplasticity—that is, the ability of the brain to rewire itself, literally changing neural pathways according to new information and skills it acquires. In other words, the brain adapts its structure to match its function.

If you value learning, mental flexibility, good memory, and the ability to be creative, then it pays to support all your brain's functions, not just the narrower ones we've come to associate with "brain exercise"—chess, listening to Mozart, or doing number puzzles, for example. More and more it seems that a strong and healthy brain and mind are the natural result of a complete lifestyle that facilitates health for the *entire* being.

"Use it or lose it" perhaps describes this phenomenon best. The brain is not a muscle, like the heart, and doesn't need to be "trained" in quite the same way. But the brain is a tool, composed of tissue and running on electrical and chemical energy that, through complex transformations, becomes our lived experience in this world.

When you fail to use your muscles, they atrophy and weaken. When you fail to use your brain, it, too, becomes less conditioned over time. That's because, as we've seen, the way we use our brain has direct physical ramifications for the way it's shaped and how it functions. In the same way as those who played Tetris for three months ended up with a brain better adapted to playing Tetris, we, too, can shape our brain according to what we want to use it for. This is the heart of neuroplasticity: The brain eventually becomes better at what it does most.

In this spirit, we can begin to think of a classic way to "train" the brain and make sure that it's putting down new, beneficial neural pathways in the way we need it to: by challenging ourselves. In this way, our brains really do have a lot in common with muscles: It's when both are pushed to the limits of their capacity that growth occurs. Challenge *stretches* us to accommodate new goals. We grow when we try to grasp something that's just on the edge of our ability—but not impossible to reach!

Most neuroscientists and psychologists now understand IQ not to be a fixed, deterministic state of affairs, but rather an inherited *range* of possible IQs for each person. Then, within that innate range, the environment and the person's own efforts decide where exactly they fall. With hard work and dedicated learning, a person can push themselves right to the edge of their natural range, and perhaps even squeeze some further performance from themselves. Similarly, a person who doesn't push themselves in this way will always have a store of untapped potential left over—they are capable of more, certainly, but their brain needs to be actively encouraged to reach those further bounds.

Much early research into IQ and cognitive science focused on how to improve a person's natural talents. We wanted to boost memory, enhance learning, find all those secret buttons that would turn us into impressive calculating machines that could effortlessly learn languages or solve complex problems through dedicated training alone. If you wanted to be better at languages, for instance, you would naturally spend time developing your linguistic abilities, right? Turns out this method may not be entirely correct.

A groundbreaking 2008 study by Jaeggi et al. showed that one could in fact increase intelligence using the right training. The researchers focused on working memory tasks, giving participants some training and then measuring them afterward to see if they improved. They did. But the more curious thing was that training on this task actually helped increase their performance *on entirely unrelated tasks*.

How could that be? How could training for one skill help people be better at a completely different skill? This research was a game changer in the field of cognitive science because it strongly suggested a model of intelligence that contrasted with our old ways of thinking about the brain. "Fluid" intelligence is not the concrete facts and skills you bank when you "learn" something new (i.e., "crystallized intelligence"). Instead, it's the flexible, adaptive *ability to learn*.

This is the brain's ability to take in, process, and store

new information. During training, whatever training it is, it's the fluid intelligence that is strengthened, and it's this *way* of thinking that transfers to other skills, explaining the surprising results of the study. The really great thing about fluid intelligence is just that—it's fluid! It can be changed through exercise and training and used across the board. And it's not about natural or inborn talent; truly it's the "use it or lose it" principle, with an added: "the more you use it, the better it is."

Essentially, improving your fluid intelligence is learning how to learn. It's practicing dealing with novel information, not just for this or that specific activity, but for activities in general. People with high fluid intelligence can thrive in a new field even with very little actual knowledge on the topic because what they possess is the optimized approach to learning, which is independent of any topic.

In fact, fluid intelligence may be closer to what we're really talking about when we discuss intelligence at all, and crystallized intelligence is more akin to knowledge, stored facts, or memory. So how do we use this finding to help our brains navigate the world better? The trick is to use a "big picture" perspective on learning in itself.

Overcoming Something: Novelty and Challenge

It's one thing to know how to respond to a stimulus you've seen a million times before, but how do you react to novel problems or ones that take a shape you've never encountered? How flexible and creative are you in adapting ideas, experimenting, truly observing what you see around you, and looking for patterns anew? This is what it means to live and think at the periphery of your abilities. While of course there's nothing wrong with training for a specific skill, there may ultimately be more to gain when you train your *total* ability to think, independent of the topic or the form your challenges take.

There are some quite startling displays of the effects of novelty and challenge on the brain. There was the time in 1970 at Cambridge University that kittens were raised in environments where they could only see horizontal or vertical lines. They were placed in cylindrical containers with either horizontal or vertical lines on the walls, never both. When caretakers took them out to feed or handle the kittens, they wore clothing that was covered in either horizontal or vertical lines. For all intents and purposes, these two groups of kittens experienced different versions of reality.

The kittens, it turned out, couldn't recognize objects or patterns of the kind that they weren't exposed to in their sealed-off environment. The kittens raised in the horizontal chambers could not see vertically aligned objects; they kept bumping into chair legs and weren't responsive when researchers thrust a finger toward them in a vertical direction. Meanwhile, the vertical cats couldn't find an appropriate place to lie down and take a nap, since they had no ability to recognize horizontal planes.

Some of the kittens in the experiment successfully rehabilitated in a few weeks, but many never did. Their primary visual cortexes had been engineered so strongly in one angle that they were effectively blind to whatever lines they weren't exposed to during those five months.

Then there is the case of taxi drivers and bus drivers in

London. Researchers from the University of London studied and compared their brain structures in 2000 and discovered something notable: The taxi drivers had measurably larger hippocampi than the bus drivers. Why might this be? The theory behind their findings was that taxi drivers had to essentially memorize the entire road map of London—they needed to know the best shortcuts and alternate courses to take, and that required in-depth knowledge about every street and alley in town. It's something that could take months or even years to learn.

The bus drivers, on the other hand, only had to drive a couple of pre-planned routes every day with little or no variation. They only needed to memorize a few turns and perhaps not even the street names. They could do this through visual memory alone, recognizing buildings or landmarks. However many people are on the bus makes no difference to the bus driver, as they already know the path and endpoint. However, being a taxi driver is somewhat like playing Russian roulette— you never know what you're going to get or how to get there. (Okay, maybe that's more Forrest Gump than Russian roulette.)

How do you practically develop a taxi driver's brain in the real world? First, get out of mental ruts. Seek novelty in situations, ideas, the people you encounter, your own thoughts. Try something new. Keep fresh eyes on old problems and ask different questions. Take a different approach from what you normally would. Seek the harder, more difficult route instead of the tried and true. Eat something different, walk a different path, ask different questions.

Second, challenge yourself. You could play it safe and

continually work at a comfortable level, and your brain will happily comply—but it's only when you push yourself a little further that you can get an idea of what you're really capable of. Pushing yourself out of your comfort zone is like a thrilling sprint across the beach at max speed—it pushes your body to its limits, and it's utterly exhilarating. In the same way, be curious about how far your brain can go. Don't be too quick to be satisfied with the status quo. Become curious; rebellious, even.

It's this curiosity that, when at its height, is almost indistinguishable from intellectual excitement, from peak performance, from joy. Being in this state of mind is a deeply creative experience. It's experiencing the wonderful unknown. Scientists and artists have this in common: they are frequently in close contact with the mysterious and are trying their best to engage it, to speak about it, to represent it, to grasp it. Creativity feeds on itself: When we can think out of the box and look at things in novel, unexpected ways, we often solve previously tricky problems or open up entirely new avenues of thought.

What this means practically is that when you're using your brain, remember to give it the opportunity to be limber so it can do what it does best. Take breaks. Unhook from intense goal-driven activity for a while to just stare out the window, to doodle, to reset or laugh or do something else for a moment. Give space for the unexpected to step in and change things for you. Take the problem apart in a different way. Creative thinking is the subject of more and more neuroscience research, but for the moment, we can take advice from those who practice it routinely: artists and other creatives.

If you're feeling blocked or mentally stale and slow, step back. Flex your brain a bit and make some open space to allow a fresh idea to enter in. Draw the problem instead of writing it. Sit somewhere else and daydream for a moment. Ask someone's opinion on the matter. Brainstorm in the shower. Have a sense of humor in completely rearranging the components of the problem in front of you, or indulge a wild fantasy in which your most fundamental assumptions about your situation are up for question (hint: they often really are.)

Creativity often comes down to the unexpected, the strange, the new. So, naturally, you won't encounter it doing the same old thing you always do! There are no rules in being creative—after all, part of the fun is making them up yourself. And remember, boosting your fluid intelligence this way means that it's transferrable. Were you encouraged to play an instrument at school? Many parents do this in the belief that learning to play will indirectly help other areas of a child's life. And they're right.

A Simple Tune

You don't need to buy an app or game that promises to boost your cognitive powers—simply pick up an instrument. Learn to read music. Master the technical skills needed to make music and practice every day. Listen to other people's creations or make your own. Musical training has been shown to be incredibly beneficial for brain health, and it engages and challenges our cognitive abilities in completely unique ways. Music builds fluid intelligence that you can "spend" elsewhere.

Playing music doesn't just take manual dexterity. It integrates our emotional experiences, our senses of vision, hearing, touch and fine motor control, memory, creative expression, and more. Brain scans in research by Gottfried Schlaug and colleagues has shown that the corpus callosum is significantly larger in musicians compared to non-musicians. This area connects the left and right hemispheres in the brain. Researchers know that it is in fact playing music that increases corpus callosum size, since those who begin with no training will show an increase over time if they train musically compared to those who do not.

What's so special about increasing the size of this part of the brain? Well, the brain always benefits from increased overall gray matter, and especially from increased connectivity *between* different regions—after all, this is how our brains work, not as static components but dynamic and interacting units that communicate constantly. Research by Agnes Chan et al. has shown that musicians outperform non-musicians on verbal, memory, and spatial reasoning tasks—there's that fluid intelligence again!

The researchers additionally found that the younger the age a person starts musical training, and the greater the intensity, the more their brains change physically to adapt. Children's brains are more plastic than adults', which is why children can benefit from even short musical lessons when they're young, even if they never go on to play in adulthood.

But if you've missed the boat, don't worry: Music training has benefits for everyone regardless of age. It may even help patients recover from stroke and other forms of brain damage, or help adults with dyslexia or other speech or learning problems. Regardless of what age you begin to play, Balbag et al. claimed in a 2014 paper that musical training can protect against the onset of dementia and neurodegenerative disease.

Specially designed brain apps and games really only train crystallized intelligence—in other words, they'll make you better able to do that *particular* task, but they won't necessarily make you more competent at other tasks. Something like music training, however, depends heavily on and improves fluid intelligence. The effects are far reaching—not to mention the increased relaxation, sense of personal accomplishment, or even the social pleasure of playing with friends.

Music is something that can tie together so many of the brain-boosting habits and techniques we've already covered. It's no exaggeration to say that musical training is one of the very best things you can do for your brain, even if it has nothing to do with your chosen area of expertise. The brain has the marvelous ability to adapt according to what it's used for. We can exploit this by making sure that we're always challenging ourselves by learning new, different skills.

Join a band, sign up for a weekly lesson in a completely new instrument, dedicate some time to learning to read music, listen to music when you can, and when you play, become aware of all the marvelous parts of your body, mind, and soul that are engaging to create this wonderful language we call music.

Bi-Lingual Madness

And speaking of languages—if you guessed that learning a new one would enhance your fluid intelligence, you'd be right. Researchers at the University of Edinburgh released an enormous study showing the link between being bilingual and reduced progression of dementia. Humans use the left hemisphere of their brain to process and store language, including specialized areas dedicated to speaking, learning new languages, and comprehending words and sounds when they're heard or read.

Language learning is a complex, whole-brain activity, however. There's so much involved: hearing the sound of a word, seeing how it's written in letters, understanding the grammar rules, knowing how to form the sound of that word correctly in your own mouth, learning how to express yourself properly, and knowing when the rules can be broken. Interestingly, where and how language is stored depends on the age at which that new knowledge is acquired. What this means is that language acquisition is not necessarily fixed and can adapt and change over the course of a lifetime.

A 2006 report compiled by Theresa Kennedy shows that learning a new language has effects on the brain's neuroplasticity—comparable to playing an instrument. Because there are so many functions involved in language learning, we get to improve so many separate areas of the brain all at once. The result is an increase in gray matter in all those areas that help us process and synthesize new information. Just as in musical training, language training increases the connections and thickness of the nerves in the corpus callosum, meaning the brain has more neural connections between the left and right hemispheres.

Whether it's learning to play the violin or chat in French, playing with the brain's plasticity not only has direct benefits for the task in front of you, but may mean you resist the onset of age-related cognitive decline and increase your performance in every other area of life where your brain is needed. Your brain isn't a fixed structure—it's alive and changing, adapting constantly to your demands and evolving with each new challenge. No matter how old you are now, it's possible to repair old neurons, create new connections, and physically alter the shape of your brain.

Keeping your brain limber and agile is not so much a matter of sitting down in front of a book or screen and forcing yourself through a dry or difficult academic exercise. It's not about any one single skill, either. Rather, a well-rounded brain is one that is fluid and responsive, able to adapt to the tasks the environment demands of it, and always with hearty doses of humor, personal significance, curiosity, and creativity. In the end, it seems like all those aspects we've typically placed to the side of the standard school curriculum—languages, music, art—are far more central to our mental well-being and intelligence than we thought.

If you only know one language, don't despair. It's the effort made to learn something new that matters. Commit to learning throughout life, in small ways every day, and your brain will not only stick around to help you, it will rise to the challenge and may even surprise you with what it can do. Leave your comfort zone and don't be afraid to make mistakes or be a beginner—it's all part of the learning process. A few minutes on a language app, a TV program in an unfamiliar language, or a new friend who can chat with you in another language might not look like supreme brain workouts, but they are!

In just the same way that eating a special superfood or

getting plastic surgery isn't the ideal strategy for improving your physical fitness, you can't expect just one trick or brain game app to drastically boost your brain power overnight. Rather, think of maintaining and developing your cognitive and intellectual health as a long-term project that you approach holistically. Keep physically, emotionally, and even spiritually healthy; give your brain plenty to do and don't be afraid to push yourself; incorporate generous rest periods; and make it a habit to engage with your creative self. In other words, support your brain, and it will support you.

If it's your memory you'd like to improve, there are now countless proven techniques and approaches that can help you study better, learn better, and simply remember more of your day-to-day life. Using mnemonics, chunking exercises, and emotional cues or varying the form new material takes (e.g., words, pictures, sounds) can all help you to remember better by working with your brain's mechanisms rather than against them.

Say It Out Loud

In 2010, Colin MacLeod and his fellow researchers explored what they named the "production effect." When they asked their participants to remember a list of words, they found that more words were remembered when the participants read some of the words out loud than if they simply read them all silently in their heads. What's so special about reading aloud? Well, probably nothing. The interesting thing is that the participants who read *all* their words out loud were actually no better off than those who studied the whole list silently.

Why on earth should reading *half* the list aloud have the best recall rate? The researchers hypothesized that doing so helped create more distinctness for the words being remembered. In other words, our brains are much better at noticing and remembering information that stands out. If you were trying to memorize a list of words and one of them was printed in red ink, while the others were in black, you almost certainly would recall that red word more easily. It's distinct. This is the same principle.

The effect the researchers discovered may come down to the fact that reading some words aloud marks these words as different somehow and more noteworthy of attention and remembering. By speaking them aloud, you're distinguishing them from the other words. The "production" in "production effect" refers to the fact that you are actively producing some words as speech, so now you have two bits of information about each word: the visual word to read quietly and the sound of the word spoken aloud.

The production effect is so useful because you are essentially expanding your knowledge about each item you need to remember, setting each of them as more distinct and clear against one another. How could you use this effect yourself when studying? Simple: pick out those very important bits of information from your material and make a point of speaking them aloud to yourself. It's likely that the conscious effort to mark out the material this way pauses your brain and tells it deliberately, "Remember this—this is important."

However, there's no reason that the production effect has to be limited to reading aloud. You can play around with exactly how you make certain bits of data in your surroundings more distinct and pertinent. Use your other senses besides sight and sound—link gestures or even emotional states to some bits of information. Literally pause in your kitchen and tell yourself out loud, with gestures, what five things you need to buy at the store. Notice how easy it is for your brain to recall this entire memory with all its quirky details when you're later walking the store aisles.

Takeaways:

- The efficacy of brain-training programs has been dispelled multiple times. This is because we can't necessarily train ourselves to be more intelligent, strictly speaking. We can, however, engage our brains in multiple and novel ways and, somewhat indirectly, become smarter as a result of that neural strengthening. We can improve our fluid intelligence, but not our crystal intelligence. This means that when we want to boost our brains, we're not really focusing on "improving" the brain itself, but rather how to stimulate it and adapt to different situations.

- The first piece of true brain training is to embrace novelty, challenge, and everything that makes you struggle a bit mentally. That's when actual neural growth is occurring—just like the gym and physical fitness, if it's not a little painful, then it's probably not doing much for your goals. This is the real foundation of improving your mental performance through neuroplasticity. A simple way to think about this is: more exposure and more experience equals more brain cells and neural connections. This can be gained in easy ways, such as changing your daily routines or rituals and simply stepping out of your comfort zone to seek more instances of unfamiliarity.

- Speaking of more neural connections, learning how to play an instrument or speak a new language literally activates dormant or underused parts of your brain. These skills provide different types of adaptations and teach you patterns and processes and how to apply them to other areas of your life. They are both truly whole-brain activities that require integrating multitudes of new information and even muscle memory. Best of all, this type of neural growth can transfer to other disciplines and practices.

- Finally, what about just reading or saying information aloud? This simple act has been shown to improve thinking, cognition, memory, and comprehension through something called the production effect. Information reproduction requires a significant amount of active participation and engagement. As is this chapter's theme, the more ways you process, engage, and challenge your brain, the more you will benefit from it.

8

THE ALMIGHTY VAGUS NERVE

You may have seen mention of the vagus nerve here and there, but what exactly is it, and what does it mean for your cognitive well-being?

Rather than being a single nerve, the vagus nerve is more like a network of nerves that runs from the back of the neck down to the abdomen. The "vagus" is Latin (and it's the same root as with words like *vagrant* and *vagabond*) and implies the nerve "wanders" throughout the body. It's really a pair of nerves, one left and right, and each very long. In fact, this network of nerves is the longest cranial nerve in our body and connects most of the major visceral organs and the brain.

The vagus nerve coordinates an incredible array of functions—and it may be even more important than we first thought. Stimulating the vagus nerve is associated with rest and relaxation, moderating our fight-or-flight response. Many now believe the mind-body connection has a lot to do with this nerve and how it can mediate between your thoughts and your feelings, your emotional state and your physical one. It's what makes people "trust their gut." In essence, it links our brains to our bodies in a significant way, and we should pay attention to something that holds such a connective power.

The fascinating thing about the vagus nerve is its relationship with the breath; it responds primarily to one's breathing rate. When we breathe slowly and deeply, we don't need our heart to pump as fast in order to supply oxygen to the rest of the body. When our breathing rate slows, it's the vagus nerve that "tells" the heart to slow down to match. Stimulating the vagus nerve directly will have this effect on the heart, which in turn calms down and relaxes our entire body, dropping our heart rate.

The opposite of the "fight-or-flight" response (the sympathetic nervous system) is the less-discussed "rest-and-digest" mode, or more technically the operation of the parasympathetic nervous system. The stress response is mediated by stress hormones like cortisol and adrenaline; the relaxation response is mediated by the breath. Suddenly, the insistence of all those Zen masters to focus on the breath begins to make sense!

This is an extremely useful piece of understanding: The relaxation response in your body can be activated directly by you, by modulating your breath. The vagus nerve will always adjust your heart rate to match your breathing. While you're not in control ordinarily of your heart rate outside of doing cardio, you *can* impact your heart rate and many more internal processes by directing your breath. Of course, this trends all the way up through the brain, reducing the cortisol and other stress hormones we experience and clearing our minds for better and more energetic thought processes.

It's a game changer. Instead of thinking your breath is

shallow and rapid *because* you're stressed, it may be more accurate to say that your body is stressing because it's obeying the message of your breath. More specifically, it's a longer exhale that triggers associated nerves that activate the relaxation response, and it's during the exhale that your vagus nerve is most "active" (i.e., when you're the most relaxed).

Professor of neurology Dr. Lucy Norcliffe-Kaufmann has been studying the vagus nerve and its effects on health since 2002. Other researchers have determined in a 2001 study that we should all be ideally breathing around six times a minute, taking five seconds in and five seconds out for each breath. Their work focuses on yoga mantras or rosary prayer—not exactly activities that you associate with brain health, but the results are there! Rosary prayer, it turns out, encourages you to breathe at about this rate, as do certain mantras. Could the secret to deep relaxation and stress relief be as simple as daily prayer and mantras?

Perhaps. The idea is to enhance what's called vagal *tone*. Though we don't often think about the health and well-being of our nerves, they can in fact show variation in tone, size, and function, and we can "train" or tone our vagus nerve much like we can tone other parts of our bodies. Again, by this point of the book, you know that we can't meaningfully compartmentalize our health, and it all trends together, so your vagal tone is a huge contributor to mental well-being and the ability to boost your brain. When we have stronger vagal tone, it means a quicker return to calm and rest and digest versus being flung all over the place and unable to regain balance.

Healthy vagus nerves are also crucial, for example, for the

management of inflammation in the body. Some inflammation is normal and healthy, but too much is associated with diseases of all kinds, such as sepsis or a host of autoimmune conditions. In a 2007 review by Kevin Tracey, we see that when the body is inflamed, cells produce a protein called TNF, or tumor necrosis factor. This is a chemical message that the vagus nerve receives, and it responds by signaling the brain to produce anti-inflammatory chemicals that downregulate the immune response. In other words, the vagus nerve is like the thermostat dialing up or down the amount of inflammation in our tissues, warding off inflammatory disease while keeping our inflammatory response in a healthy range.

But this is just one of the many wonderful roles the vagus nerve plays. It turns out that it can also literally help you make memories. Researchers from the University of Virginia have found that vagus nerve stimulation actively improves memory. The vagus nerve is responsible for modulating the release of norepinephrine, which is known to consolidate memories in the amygdala. This has interesting implications for those trying to boost their brain power: Relaxation improves memory, while stress impairs it.

The vagus nerve also stimulates the release of another important neurotransmitter, acetylcholine, which is involved in telling your lungs to breathe. A detailed review by Piccioto and colleagues outlines acetylcholine's complicated relationship with the rest of the body—and with the vagus nerve. This is why some people recommend toning your vagus nerve by practicing holding your breath for up to eight counts, making shallow breaths a thing of the past.

The vagus nerve doesn't only communicate via neurotransmitter, but can "talk" to the heart by sending electrical impulses to its own inbuilt "pacemaker." Acetylcholine plays a crucial role in interacting with this region in the heart, thereby slowing its rate, according to a 2010 paper by Huston and Tracey. In fact, doctors can get an idea of your vagus nerve health (and your heart health!) by measuring your heart rate variability, or HRV.

It's clear to most neuroscientists that the humble vagus nerve has widespread and vital functions throughout the body. Boosting vagal tone is not just great for encouraging relaxation and cutting stress, it has measurable benefits on heart health, breathing, and your memory function, to name just a few.

So, how do we tone the vagal nerve and start reaping these benefits?

First, the bad news: there is some genetic predisposition to vagal nerve tone, but the good news is that there is a lot you can do to boost it yourself. It doesn't cost anything and it's not difficult—but it does take persistent and regular practice.

The first technique we've already addressed: deep, rhythmic breathing. When it comes to effective deep-breathing maneuvers, *any* type of deep, slow diaphragmatic breathing—during which you visualize filling up the lower part of your lungs just above your belly button like a balloon . . . and then exhaling slowly—is going to stimulate your vagus nerve, activate your parasympathetic nervous system, and improve your HRV.

Breathe from the diaphragm, breathe slowly, and breathe evenly. Focus and count each breath, too, and you'll discover that you'll easily put yourself in a state not dissimilar from deep meditation. Breathe as you go about your day. Breathe when you get up, when you go to sleep. Take a moment as often as you can to tune in. This may wind up being way more beneficial than a dedicated meditation session that you only pull off once in a while.

Some people make time every day to practice diaphragmatic breathing as part of a yoga or mindfulness-meditation routine. Others only take a really deep breath anytime they catch themselves feeling "panicky," need to find grace under pressure, or want to relieve some frustration. All of these applications of diaphragmatic breathing can reap huge benefits. Some diaphragmatic breathing techniques prescribe inhaling and exhaling only via mouth breathing. Other experts recommend breathing only through your nose. Try using a combination of both. You can also inhale very slowly through the nose, as deeply as possible until your lungs feel like they will explode, and then blow the air right back out through pursed lips in a consistent stream. In the end, you should contract your abdominal muscles to empty your body of all air . . . and then do it again. Again, practice whatever type of diaphragmatic breathing fits your lifestyle and feels right.

Remember, the goal is twofold: to be able to fall back on this type of breathing in all instances and calm yourself, and also increase your vagal tone on a consistent basis so your fight-or-flight response is not so easily provoked.

It's reassuring to have fresh research corroborate that each of us can trigger a "relaxation response" (Benson et al., 1975) simply by focusing on the inhalation-to-exhalation ratio of our breathing and consciously extending the length of each exhale while doing breathing exercises as we go about our day-to-day lives.

Humming is another technique that can increase vagus nerve tone. Mechanically stimulating the vocal chords inadvertently stimulates the vagus nerve that connects to them—the voice box, to be specific. You could even combine a quiet chant to yourself with your breathing exercise. The same vocal nerves can be activated by speaking or singing. On top of this stimulation, humming requires you to control your inhalations and exhalations. Experts know that, even without humming, the vagus nerve links to respiration, and slowing down exhalation has a calming effect, activating the parasympathetic nervous system.

Another technique is to wash your face with cold water. The exact reason this works is still poorly understood, but it may have something to do with the "mammalian diving reflex," an ancient evolutionary vestige that originally served to lower our heart rate when we'd need to hold our breath, i.e., when swimming underwater. It may also function similarly to cold showers, which initially send the body into a state of shock and panic—but with practice, you can learn to control your impulses and calm yourself down intentionally and through sheer will.

If deep breathing and chanting sound suspiciously like meditation to you, well, a 2018 study by Gerritson and Band found meditation does indeed enhance vagal tone. "Contemplative activity," focus on the breath, and loving kindness meditation don't only make you feel calmer and kinder to your fellow human beings, they may literally alter the structure of your vagus nerve, not to mention positively affect every aspect of your body.

Finally, the all-important gut-brain connection (including the vagus nerve) is improved by ensuring gut bacteria are healthy, so if you don't already take a probiotic or eat fermented foods on occasion, now is a great time to start.

And just like that, we arrive again unavoidably at the brain-body-spirit connection. The vagus nerve shows us that the links between these different aspects of our being are not abstract—they're literal. Importantly, the relationship is dynamic and bidirectional: These components interact with each other in complex ways, establishing feedback loops that, in aggregate, create our overall sense of well-being (or *un*well-being, for that matter!).

Though we began this book exploring all the ways the physical brain can be supported to enhance our memory and overall cognition, we find ourselves considering practices like meditation, rest, and even prayer as ways to benefit our health, no less effective than working out or taking supplements. Thus, the suspicion that physical health is not at all separate from mental health is confirmed, with research showing time again that our physical bodies are shaped by our mindset, daily behaviors, and focus. By harnessing these natural feedback mechanisms, you can use regular daily practice to ensure you're living your calmest, happiest, most effective self in each moment—not just cognitively but in every sense.

A practical suggestion: next time you are overwhelmed, sad, stressed, alone, or unwell, simply stop and take a moment to breathe properly. It doesn't matter whether you visualize this as a cleansing breath that recharges your spirit, or if you dwell on the science of the respiratory nerves that you stimulate—simply stop and breathe slowly and deeply. Combine this practice with meditation, contemplation, or visualization. Pair it with a meaningful mantra like, "I'm okay. I can do this. All is well." Spend extra time on the exhale. This can be done before a nerve-wracking presentation, after a breakup, in heavy traffic, or before a panic attack strikes.

Remember the link between the vagus nerve and your heart rate? Because the connection is so close, improving the vagus nerve helps heart health—and boosting heart health improves the vagus nerve. So, take care of your heart. You already know you need to exercise, but make sure you're including plenty of cardio in the mix. Strive for a lower resting heart rate, which naturally leads to a well-toned vagus nerve, and as always, opt for a heart-healthy diet.

Knowing what you now know about the vagus nerve, make an effort to literally trust your gut more. Practice meditation daily, even for short periods, and make a habit of tuning in to your physical sensations and nurturing that body awareness and mind-body connection. Vague feelings and intuitions are not groundless—they are often the corporeal sensations that have been sent to your higher brain by your vagus nerve. Literally: listen to your gut!

In keeping with the ongoing importance of relaxation, remember to build in plenty of time every day for rest and downtime, doing nothing in particular. Encourage a state of "rest and digest" whenever you can. This could be a self-care ritual, therapy, sleep, time spent with family, or anything that allows you to let go and slow down. With time, you can start to view any stressful or challenging situation in life as a valuable opportunity for emotional mastery—except this time, you'll be approaching the problem not from a purely psychological perspective, but with an understanding that your *entire being* is involved.

The wonderful thing about working with your vagus nerve is the understanding that your consciousness can in fact be in control at any time. No matter how stressed you feel, how out of control, or how low, you can always stop, take a breath, and do something objectively healthy for you.

This means that many of the tricks and activities we typically associate with emotional and spiritual health—such as visualization and meditation—in fact have demonstrable physical effects and can be as beneficial for our physical health as good diet and exercise. For example, the next time you're under pressure or feeling upset or stressed, pause to literally visualize your vagus nerve. Talk to it, even. Visualize your entire body calming down in whatever way seems appealing to you—picture a soothing golden light washing over you, envision your nerves as ropes that are literally slackening and loosening, or imagine with each exhale you are releasing tensions and worrisome thoughts with the breath.

The wonderful thing about developing and nurturing whole-body wellness is that you are entirely at liberty to do what works for you. You don't have to divide yourself up into components—your body requiring such-and-such intervention, your mind demanding a separate approach, and so on. Rather, there are only healthful activities that support our total, dynamic wellness—healthy habits that are not tacked onto life as an afterthought but built into the very way we live every day and each moment.

So, combine a self-care ritual like a hot bath with meditation, develop a daily journaling habit, or spend every evening taking a walk in nature with friends—an activity that boosts your cardiovascular health, activates your vagus nerve, and strengthens your emotional connections to those you love, adding meaning and depth to life. When you're at work or studying, take it easy, safe with the knowledge that forcing yourself through unpleasant work will not make you any smarter or your memory any sharper. Instead, relax often, knowing it's this loose, unstructured time that will help your brain, creativity, and intellect be the best it can be. You'll be all the better prepared to challenge yourself when necessary!

Keep a fine balance in your life between action and inaction, between boredom and challenge, between sleep and waking. Paradoxically, we perform best when we seek not high accomplishment and the extremes of achievement, but rather holistic balance. Living this way not only yields better results, it *feels* better. Make positive thinking, mantras, and meditation a non-negotiable part of a healthy lifestyle, just as important as drinking water and eating your veggies.

Support your neuroplasticity by getting out there and enjoying life, trying new things, learning, changing your mind, evolving. Exercise is good for you, but who says it has to be in a sterile, boring gym where you run in place on a treadmill? Why not instead hike up a challenging mountain and give your artistic side a workout at the top by taking some creative pictures of the view? We all know how important the right foods are for our memory and cognitive health, but that doesn't mean we can't also use healthy food as a means of expression, a challenging hobby, a way to connect with loved ones, or even a method to participate meaningfully in one's culture and heritage.

Using meditation, rest, creativity, and social interaction to rewire your vagus nerve is not only possible, it's smart. Have you ever noticed that some people seem to do certain things with so much more ease than others? Perhaps you went to school with a student who didn't seem to study all that hard and wasn't exactly super intelligent, and yet they performed well on tests despite not having studied as much as others. What such students might have inadvertently discovered is all the other ways to support brain health that don't look like slaving over a book or drawing mind maps.

If you're trying to optimize your brain, look at the rest of your life and ask whether you are doing enough to support your cognitive abilities. Examine your daily schedule and make a more conscious effort to include plenty of dynamic exercise, social engagements, challenging and meaningful work, enough water, sleep, good food eaten in good company, and as always, as many creative and out-of-the-box solutions as you can muster to the ordinary problems of daily life.

Picture your vagus nerve—and your entire nervous system—as a kind of emotional and mental regulatory system. Think carefully about how you're going to be active in managing stress levels. Quitting a draining job, avoiding people who worsen your mood, or taking up a completely unrelated hobby are not the first things you might imagine when trying to improve your intellectual capacity, but they may ultimately do more for you than number puzzles or forcing yourself to listen to classical music if it bores you!

Takeaways:

- The vagus nerve is the embodiment of the phrase "mind-body connection." Why is that? Because that's what it literally does. It's a cranial nerve that runs through the entire body, and through some smart manipulation, we can use this nerve to actually change what is happening in the brain. The vagus nerve demonstrates that sometimes the brain follows what the body experiences, and this is another angle through which we can boost our brain.
- The vagus nerve corresponds strongly with what you might call the relaxation response, or rest-and-digest mode, which stands in stark contrast to fight-or-flight or panic mode (and all the associated neurotransmitters and hormones with both types of modes). If you have weak vagal tone, then you will fall prey to anxiety and stress easily; if you can strengthen your vagal tone (yes, similar to a physical muscle), then you'll have a tendency to recover more quickly from stressful situations and regulate yourself better.
- The question becomes: how can you strengthen your vagal tone? The most prominent way is to work on deep, diaphragmatic breathing, as breath is one of the vagus nerve's key regulators. The more slowly and deeply you can breathe, the more you can summon this rest-and-digest mode and

relax. In fact, making noises such as humming, chanting, or praying also invokes the same effect, as the vagus nerve is connected to the voice box and larynx. You can also practice splashing yourself (start with the face) with cold water, as it briefly evokes your fight-or-flight response but then allows you to practice summoning your rest-and-digest response.

- The vagus nerve makes it clear that you have the ability to control your physical response, thus giving your brain the chance to think at peak performance. The vagus nerve is also the embodiment of the inseparable nature of the brain and the body. As the vagus nerve shows us, to boost your brain, you must focus on everything that supports and surrounds it.

SUMMARY GUIDE

Chapter 1. Neurofitness

- Physical fitness begets neurofitness. It may be tempting to separate the two, but in truth, they are inexorably linked to your optimized thinking and functioning. We may not be able to specifically train the brain, but by training our bodies in specific ways, we can effect the changes that we want.

- The first step to physical fitness is to work up a sweat on a regular basis. Of note, this should be aerobic exercise that gets your blood pumping and your heart rate up. This also increases the blood flow to your brain, kicks off a host of metabolic and hormonal changes, and energizes you. It's been shown that aerobic exercise can increase the size of parts of our brains responsible for higher cognitive functions and memory, and can even fight cognitive decline and brain diseases. The brain is a hungry, hungry organ, so we should make sure the systems that feed it are optimized and healthy.

- Yoga and dance have also been found to be effective in increasing neurofitness. This may be surprising because they are not strictly seen as aerobic activities. Sure, dance can be as strenuous as running, but part of the benefit with these modes of exercise is the ability to express emotions in a gratifying way. This is demonstrated by the fact that these modes do a lot to battle and prevent depression and anxiety. How often are we able to truly unplug, let go, express ourselves, or reflect upon our lives? The links are not one hundred percent definitive, but the benefits have been documented time after time, so perhaps the "why" is not as important as the "how."

- Emotional wellness and calmness are a train of thought that makes one think of mindfulness and meditation, and it turns out that these methods do provide some of the same avenues to brain boosting. The restorative power of dance and yoga actually uncovers another rabbit hole we will dive into later: self-care.

Chapter 2. Neurotransmitter Fine-tuning

- Neurotransmitters are the brain's chemical messengers, and there are four major types, called DOSE chemicals, that greatly influence our overall experience: dopamine, oxytocin, serotonin, and endorphins.
- Oxytocin is the love hormone responsible for feelings of bonding, connection, empathy, and safety. You can increase oxytocin by consciously fostering trust in your social network and being more trustworthy yourself. Think in terms of service, relationships, and interdependence and strategically trust those around you to create warm connections.

- Serotonin is a mood stabilizer and "confidence hormone," which is all about self-esteem, self-determination, and competence. To increase serotonin levels, believe in yourself, confidently assert boundaries, have the courage to lead, and dwell on your achievements rather than your failures.

- Endorphins are the brain's natural painkillers and mitigate anxiety and depression, boost self-esteem, modulate appetite, and even enhance immune response. To increase it, we can try vigorous exercise, spicy foods, stretching, or laughing.

- Dopamine is the brain's reward molecule and involves the anticipation of future pleasure, which cements our habits. We can create more dopamine any time we set a new goal for ourselves and reward ourselves with every baby step toward that goal.

- If you battle with addiction, a dopamine detox or fast might help. Try to avoid or remove the triggering stimulus, but when you inevitably encounter it, practice "urge surfing" and facing discomfort without succumbing. Reconnect to your values to replace the compulsive behavior with something that genuinely brings benefit to your life instead.

Chapter 3. A Brainy Routine

- For our purposes, a daily routine is simply a set of actions you can implement to consistently improve your brain health and mental performance. Taken together, these are all helpful for your mental hygiene, and even more so when they become your unconscious habits and natural pattern of behavior.

- We must start with a good night's sleep, as it is the basis for everything. Without sleep, there is no energy, and there is nothing else your brain can devote attention to. Sleep, and even frequent napping, is a force multiplier; this means that it alone is an enormous catalyst to either improve your daily mental performance or flush it down the toilet. Give it the respect it deserves; it's not only about your energy levels, but there are very real neurological changes in the face of sleep debt.

- Surprisingly (or not), nature alone has great power. And this is not in the sense that natural disasters such as hurricanes and earthquakes can alter our lives. There is tremendous influence in simply seeing green foliage, exposing yourself to natural light, having plants in your workspace, and even looking at pictures or videos of animals. The exact mechanism by which this helps us is not known, but it is theorized that nature simply grounds us and reduces our stress to a place where we can focus better. It causes us to be more mindful and aware of our surroundings, mood, and place in the world.

- Some simple actions can also work in the same way to concentrate our efforts and ground us. Chewing gum and doodling while you are thinking or speaking has been shown to improve memory and focus.

- Finally, the practice of daily gratitude has been shown to increase happiness, focus, and even energy. Unlike the other elements of daily routines in this chapter, gratitude consciously grounds you and makes you think about your actions more intentionally, and there are real hormonal and biological changes as a result.

Chapter 4. The Social Brain

- Our identities do not come in a vacuum; we identify ourselves largely by our background, culture, and upbringing. These are all aspects of our social nature as humans: Humans are social animals, and this means that other people are an essential part of our healthy functioning and happiness. This is no different for our brains.

- Sex has been shown to improve cognitive functioning as well as overall life satisfaction and happiness (no surprise on this one). But it's a blurry assertion that the pure mechanical act of sex itself improves brain health—it is likely instead tied to the emotional, social bonding, and supportive aspects that often go hand in hand with sex. In any case, deny yourself of this natural and primal human urge to your detriment.

- On a grander scale, socialization and interaction have been shown to improve mental faculties and also battle cognitive decline in elderly people. How much is enough? That is a personal matter, but there are ways to seek out social interaction in daily life if you look for it. You might even say that without sufficient social interaction, you are depriving the brain of a need just like you would be if you had poor sleep hygiene.

- Annoyingly, just like all those inspirational posters will preach, laughter really *is* one of the best medicines.

- A surprising entry here is the power of thinking about your ancestors. It's been shown that simply pausing a moment to think about those who came before you can improve cognitive performance. Why is that? It's a social activity but not quite an interaction, yet this type of thinking has a sort of gravity that humbles you and brings perspective. More importantly, it makes you focus and concentrate on the task at hand by virtue of minimizing the importance of things that are not actually important (not an easy task in itself).

Chapter 5. Mental Sabbatical

- Sometimes a mental sabbatical is just what you need. Actually, this should be an essential part of your daily, weekly, and monthly routine. We all need to disconnect and recharge; our brains are incapable of functioning at a high level without that rest. Consider this chapter in combination with the chapter on neurofitness, and once again, the holistic mind-body connection cannot be ignored and must be cultivated.

- When it comes to relaxing, there are a few methods that run counter to what you might assume is most helpful. Some people just want to turn into a vegetable on the couch, and that works to a certain degree. But video games, television, and reading are all excellent ways of combining rest, relaxation, and beneficial mental engagement. They all emphasize different modes of thought—video games force you to adapt to quicker reaction speeds and problem-solving; reading and television allow you to inhabit the minds of others. The media itself is not important, actually; it's just that it is pleasurable mental engagement that leaves you feeling better about yourself after the fact.

- Practicing meditation and mindfulness is the most predictable tip for relaxation. Stop ruminating on the past or the future. Try to not even focus on the present. Attempt to clear your mind and think only about one thing, such as your breathing. It sounds like the easiest thing in the world, and yet, you'll struggle to do it. But pursuing this seemingly tiny goal will result in massive neurological changes that will improve your resistance to stress and anxiety and wire your system for more resilience.

Chapter 6. Protect Your Brain from Stress

- It is difficult if not impossible to maintain healthy, resilient brain health in the face of chronic stress. Ongoing low-grade stress is associated with mental illness and can literally damage the structures of the brain for the long term. Stress can kill newly formed brain cells and even lead to brain shrinkage, as well as interfere with memory.
- One way to reduce stress is by learning to control arousal via breath control. Deep belly breathing can lower central nervous system arousal and regulate stress levels, protecting our brain.
- Try simply focusing on slow, deep, and controlled breathing for a few moments, or practice the more energizing "lion's breath" yogic exercise, the soothing and balancing "humming bee" practice, or the mind-clearing Navy SEAL "box breathing" technique.
- Another important way to manage the body's stress response is to become mindful of your thoughts and emotions, and

challenge and rewrite distorted thoughts patterns that are creating stress for you.

- One proven method is affect labeling, or putting words to the emotion you're feeling. This can create psychological distance, distract you, allow you a reappraisal of the situation, and even change how you act in response. Simply notice without judgment how you're feeling, write it down, or share your observation with others in conversations.

- You can also reframe certain thoughts and counteract the innate human negativity bias. The brain is neuroplastic and can be trained to interpret neutral stimuli differently. First become aware of a negative thought and then compare it against your values, your goals, and any objective evidence, opting if necessary for a healthier alternative that is less distorted.

Chapter 7. True Brain Training

- The efficacy of brain-training programs has been dispelled multiple times. This is because we can't necessarily train ourselves to be more intelligent, strictly speaking. We can, however, engage our brains in multiple and novel ways and, somewhat indirectly, become smarter as a result of that neural strengthening. We can improve our fluid intelligence, but not our crystal intelligence. This means that when we want to boost our brains, we're not really focusing on "improving" the brain itself, but rather how to stimulate it and adapt to different situations.

- The first piece of true brain training is to embrace novelty, challenge, and everything that makes you struggle a bit mentally. That's when actual neural growth is occurring—just like the gym and physical fitness, if it's not a little painful, then it's probably not doing much for your goals. This is the real foundation of improving your mental performance through neuroplasticity. A simple way to think about this is: more exposure and more experience equals more brain cells and neural connections. This can be gained in easy ways, such as changing your daily routines or rituals and simply stepping out of your comfort zone to seek more instances of unfamiliarity.

- Speaking of more neural connections, learning how to play an instrument or speak a new language literally activates dormant or underused parts of your brain. These skills provide different types of adaptations and teach you patterns and processes and how to apply them to other areas of your life. They are both truly whole-brain activities that require integrating multitudes of new information and even muscle memory. Best of all, this type of neural growth can transfer to other disciplines and practices.

- Finally, what about just reading or saying information aloud? This simple act has been shown to improve thinking, cognition, memory, and comprehension through something called the production effect. Information reproduction requires a significant amount of active participation and engagement. As is this chapter's theme, the more ways you process, engage, and challenge your brain, the more you will benefit from it.

Chapter 8. The Almighty Vagus Nerve

- The vagus nerve is the embodiment of the phrase "mind-body connection." Why is that? Because that's what it literally does. It's a cranial nerve that runs through the entire body, and through some smart manipulation, we can use this nerve to actually change what is happening in the brain. The vagus nerve demonstrates that sometimes the brain follows what the body experiences, and this is another angle through which we can boost our brain.

- The vagus nerve corresponds strongly with what you might call the relaxation response, or rest-and-digest mode, which stands in stark contrast to fight-or-flight or panic mode (and all the associated neurotransmitters and hormones with both types of modes). If you have weak vagal tone, then you will fall prey to anxiety and stress easily; if you can strengthen your vagal tone (yes, similar to a physical muscle), then you'll have a tendency to recover more quickly from stressful situations and regulate yourself better.

- The question becomes: how can you strengthen your vagal tone? The most prominent way is to work on deep, diaphragmatic breathing, as breath is one of the vagus nerve's key regulators. The more slowly and deeply you can breathe, the more you can summon this rest-and-digest mode and relax. In fact, making noises such as humming, chanting, or praying also invokes the same effect, as the vagus nerve is connected to the voice box and larynx. You can also practice splashing yourself (start with the face) with cold water, as it briefly evokes your fight-or-flight response but then allows you to practice summoning your rest-and-digest response.

- The vagus nerve makes it clear that you have the ability to control your physical response, thus giving your brain the chance to think at peak performance. The vagus nerve is also the embodiment of the inseparable nature of the brain and the body. As the vagus nerve shows us, to boost your brain, you must focus on everything that supports and surrounds it.